KEYS TO UNDERSTANDING SECURITIES

Second Edition

Anita Jones Lee
Austin Lynas
Janet Lowe

BARRON'S

© Copyright 2000 Barron's Educational Series, Inc.
Prior © Copyright 1989 by Barron's Educational Series, Inc.

All inquiries should be addressed to:
Barron's Educational Series, Inc.
250 Wireless Boulevard
Hauppauge, NY 11788
http://www.barronseduc.com

Library of Congress Catalog Card Number 00-36009

International Standard Book Number 0-7641-1309-7

Library of Congress Cataloging-in-Publication Data

Jones-Lee, Anita.
    Keys to understanding securities / Anita Jones Lee, Austin Lynas, Janet Lowe. — 2nd ed.
        p.   cm. — (Barron's business keys)
    Includes index.
    ISBN 0-7641-1309-7
    1. Securities—United States. I. Lynas, Austin. II. Lowe, Janet.
III. Title. IV. Series.
HG4910.L446   2000
332.63'2—dc21   00-036009
                                            CIP

TABLE OF CONTENTS

INTRODUCTION

This is a book about some of the financial products and basic concepts that have become a part of the everyday language in the fields of securities law and analysis.

New financial products are being developed so rapidly that many experts and sellers of these products, let alone the less sophisticated consumers of the products, find it increasingly difficult to get beyond the jargon to understand just what is being sold. Adding to the problem is the dazzling variety of securities traded in national markets today: common stocks, preferreds, CATS, TIGERS, LYONS, convertible bonds, Ginnie Maes, and so on form an endless parade of esoterica seemingly designed to befuddle and bewilder. Although you may not need to master the structures of every security on the market today before investing, you do need to know the right questions to ask. The 44 Keys in this book should help you do just that.

This book presents some of the major legal and analytic features of securities used by lawyers and securities analysts in dealing with the investing public. It can be used as a primer for those who have little background in either securities law or securities analysis and who desire a relatively brief one-stop introduction to the basic concepts of these fields. For those with more extensive backgrounds in securities, the book can be used as a memory jogger and as a complement to the training given newer staff members.

A complete presentation of securities laws and the theories of securities analysis is beyond the space limitations in this introductory book. To begin to achieve a more comprehensive understanding of the legal structure and analytic features of securities, the following books should be helpful to you:

1. *The Intelligent Investor* by Benjamin Graham

2. *Handbook of Investment Products and Services* by Victor Harper
3. *Securities Law Handbook* by Harold Bloomenthal
4. *Barron's Dictionary of Finance and Investment Terms* by John Downs and Jordan Goodman
5. *The Warren Buffett Portfolio* by Robert Hagstrom
6. *Value Investing Made Easy* by Janet Lowe

Throughout the book, we try to use the most widely accepted definitions of the securities products and concepts discussed. Although the current vogue among investment firms of giving their own private labels to variations of products sharing the same basic design complicates this task, we have adopted the approach of erring on the side of using generic names where possible and private labels only where necessary to further your understanding.

The progression of the book is more or less from the basic securities, such as common stock and bonds, to the more complex financial products, such as convertible securities, pass-through securities, and other more structured products. In Key 36 we describe several investment scams. By telling you about some of the storied swindles of the past and arming you with the proper vocabulary and questions to ask of securities promoters, this Key should help you avoid falling for similar scams. Also included is an overview of the major federal securities laws and the basics of securities transfer. The later Keys describe the principal theories of securities valuation that have dominated the marketplace for the last half century.

The Keys on securities valuation (Keys 15 through 19) are included to give you an appreciation for the styles of investing that others have used successfully. These Keys will help you to identify which valuation theories make sense and to categorize the type of strategy you or your broker is following. You may be surprised to learn that you disagree with the fundamental theories your broker/adviser uses to guide investments of your money.

1

WHAT IS A SECURITY?

What is or is not a security is an open, and often hotly argued, legal question. A detective setting out to discover among the volumes of history on securities the true meaning of the word "security" would find that the trail ends just about where it began. Much of the content of the definition is circular. Much depends on context and circumstance. For example, of the six basic federal securities statutes, four of them (The 33 Act, The Trust Indenture Act of 1939, The Investment Company Act of 1940, and The Investment Advisors Act of 1940) define a security to mean "any note...bond...evidence of indebtedness...collateral trust certificate...investment contract...or, in general, any interest or instrument commonly known as a 'security' or any certificate of interest or participation in...any of the foregoing."

As we will see later, securities are regulated and defined on many levels, and the answer to the question "What is a security?" may depend not only on the laws involved but also on the policies motivating those laws. Narrowing the scope to federal law and policy, we find it useful to break the basic statutory definition into three areas: investment contracts, commonly known securities, and notes and bonds.

Investment Contracts. Forty years ago, the Supreme Court in the case of *SEC v. Howey* tried to settle the issue of when an *investment contract* is a security by declaring that a security is a contract made between parties to share profits from a common effort. That case shows how the policy of protecting investors from sharp tactics has influenced the derivation of a definition of a security as an *investment contract.*

The Howey Company owned a resort hotel in a scenic section of Florida adjacent to fine orange groves. As patrons of the hotel were escorted around the Florida countryside surrounding the resort, their attention was drawn to the orange trees and they were told that parcels of land in the groves were for sale. If they indicated an interest, they were given a sales talk and offered two contracts, a land sales contract from the Howey Company, and a service contract from Howey-in-the-Hills Service, Inc., which cultivated, harvested, and marketed the crops.

Although the purchasers of the land sales contract were free to use any service company, the salesmen stressed the superiority of Howey-in-the-Hills. Not surprisingly, 85 percent of the land sold by Howey over a three-year period ending May 31, 1943 was also serviced by Howey-in-the-Hills. Once signed, the service contract bound the purchaser for 10 years without an option for cancellation, gave Howey-in-the-Hills full and complete possession of the land, and denied the purchaser the right to enter the land to market the crop unless the purchaser obtained the consent of Howey-in-the-Hills. Thus, the balance of power in the contract was tilted heavily in favor of the Howey companies. Added to this imbalanced equation was the troubling profile of most purchasers. As the Supreme Court observed, "The purchasers for the most part are nonresidents of Florida. They are predominantly business and professional people who lack the knowledge, skill, and equipment necessary for the care and cultivation of citrus trees. They are attracted by the expectations of profits."

The Court held that the orange grove contract constituted a security within the meaning of the federal securities laws because it met a three-part test of an "investment contract."

1. A contract, transaction, or scheme whereby a person invests his money in

2

2. a common enterprise and
3. is led to expect profits solely from the efforts of a promoter or a third party.

The commerce clause of the U.S. Constitution gives Congress the authority to regulate practices or activity using mails or other instrumentalities of interstate commerce such as the telephone. Because the Howey sales force admittedly used instrumentalities of interstate commerce, there was no question that the orange grove contracts could be regulated federally. Also, since a single letter mailed or telephone call placed constitutes a use of an instrumentality of interstate commerce, stumbling into the ambit of federal securities regulation is, as a general matter, about as easy as breathing.

In the wake of *Howey,* courts have interpreted *security* broadly to include all of the instruments commonly regarded in commerce as securities as well as novel instruments if they meet the three-part Howey test. In the often cited words of the Supreme Court, the concept of a security "embodies a flexible rather than a static principle, one that is capable of adaptation to meet the countless and variable schemes devised by those who seek the use of the money of others on the promise of profits."

That is, determining whether a particular financial instrument qualifies as an investment contract and therefore a security essentially involves a facts-and-circumstances analysis. One of the keys to understanding what constitutes a security is to remember that courts generally have interpreted the term security as broadly as is necessary to effect the general purpose and policies of the securities law in order to protect investors from deceptive, sharp, or otherwise unlawful practices. And remember that, to qualify as a security, an instrument or arrangement need only fit within one of the categories of the statutory definition. The second major category of the statutory definition of securities are instruments "commonly known as securities."

Instruments Commonly Known as Securities. Through admittedly circular in definition, this category is useful because a number of instruments and arrangements have almost universally come to be regarded as securities in federal, state, and international contexts. The common stock, bonds, and certificates of companies traded on national or international exchanges are examples of such securities-by-reputation.

In fact, without benefit of an exact legal definition, financial products understood to be securities have existed for many centuries, and examples abound of faddish buying and selling manias. For example, during the South Sea Bubble scandal of the 1700s (more on this and other scams in Key 36), much of the population of England is believed to have owned South Sea Company securities before that stock crashed in 1720. The key elements to the concept then are the same ones important to the federal securities laws today: schemes or arrangements sold broadly to the public, purchasers who have little or no direct control over the company in which they invest and who thus rely on the efforts of other persons to create profits. For, unlike yesterday's blacksmith and son, who together would shoe horses and divide up the profits at the end of the day, the basic feature—perhaps the key feature—of securities is that they permit the separation of *control* of the production of a product from the *ownership* of the product. No moral tone is intended here. Separation of control from ownership is neither necessarily bad nor good, but the existence of the separation explains the need for many of the regulations we'll examine later.

Notes, Collateral Trust Certificates, and Others. In addition to covering securities-by-reputation and those instruments and arrangements meeting the *Howey* definition of an investment contract, the federal statutes also sweep into the definition of security products on an illustrative list, such as notes, bonds, and collateral trust certificates. Notes and bonds are IOUs issued by companies

4

to purchasers who become, in effect, creditors of the company. Collateral trust certificates are instruments issued to purchasers representing a fraction of the ownership of the assets of a trust, say one third. The underlying asset of the trust can be houses or cars or orange groves or any other type of property. Though the one-third investor in the trust owns the part of the assets of the trust represented by the fraction bought, he or she doesn't actually have a third of a house or a third of an orange grove, but instead receives a certificate representing the fractional ownership interest. The security therefore is, to use a phrase of the late Speaker of the House of Representatives Sam Rayburn, a "symbol of ownership." And the purchasers are owners of these symbols.

We make three assumptions throughout this book.

1. Although the determination of whether a given instrument constitutes a security depends on an analysis that does not always yield clear-cut answers, throughout, when we speak of securities we mean those instruments or arrangements that, in the context sold, would constitute securities within the meaning of the federal securities laws.

2. When we speak of nongovernment securities, you can assume that corporations are the issuers of the securities, though securities can be, and often are, issued by other business forms such as partnerships.

3. Corporations are assumed, where such an assumption is necessary, to be subject to federal securities laws. The various state securities laws are a matter for another book.

2

TYPES OF SECURITIES

Securities can be divided into many categories. Each category should be thought of as a separate question to be posed in your analysis of a security prior to making an investment. Securities may be grouped, among other ways, in the following categories.

1. Debt or equity
2. Rated or unrated
3. Single-class or multiple-class
4. Having special rights against the company or not
5. Having credit enhancements or not
6. Government or corporate

Debt/Equity. A *debt security* represents a loan from the investor, as creditor, to the issuing company, as debtor. The Keys dealing with debt securities (see Keys 28 through 32) will help you to identify the most common forms of debt securities, whether the securities are unsecured loans or whether they are backed by collateral in some form, and the approach you should use in evaluating the quality of the debt security. Common debt securities include debentures, bonds, and government securities. Most of the considerations associated with making a loan to a company apply equally to investing in debt securities. The payoff to the investor comes in the form of interest, and the potential for profit is thus rather fixed. Once the company pays off the loan you have made to it, it has no further obligation to you, and you are not entitled to share further in the wealth of the company.

An *equity security* represents ownership. Equity securities include common stock and many forms of pass-through securities (see Keys 24 and 26). These securities may be further divided according to whether they represent ownership in the company issuing the security or in specific assets of the company. Because they represent ownership, equity securities give you the means of sharing the wealth of a company's performance. All of us have heard of the fabulous growth of companies such as Microsoft, Walmart, and General Electric. Early investors in these companies reaped fortunes.

Rated/Unrated. Securities, whether they are debt or equity, may also be divided into rated securities or unrated securities. Rated securities have been assigned a rating by a rating agency such as Standard & Poor's, Moody's, or Duff & Phelps. Ratings give you one indication of whether the company or institution that issued the security is in good financial health. Companies with poor or failing indications may be placed on a watch list and/or may suffer a decline in ratings. In Key 35, we review the criteria the major ratings agencies use in deriving their ratings for debt securities and for common stock. You should familiarize yourself with the basic mechanics of arriving at the ratings so that you will understand when a security or a company in which you have invested is showing signs of financial illness.

Single-Class/Multiple-Class. Another way to guide your analysis of securities is to check whether the security is a single-class security or whether it is only one of a multiple-class issuance. This distinction is important because it will help you to judge whether your rights as a security holder may be prejudiced by the rights of the holders of other classes of securities that may rank ahead of your security in terms of payment rights, voting rights, bankruptcy rights, or other rights.

Special Rights. Certain special rights against the issuing company may greatly enhance the value of a security by providing added insurance against financial misfortune. For example, in several of the Keys that follow, we discuss *put rights,* which give the security holder the right to sell the security back to the issuing company under certain circumstances. Another special right the security may carry is the right to exchange the security for a different security of the company. These rights of *convertibility* may, for example, enable you to trade debt securities for an equivalent value of equity securities after a certain period of time.

Credit Enhancements. Securities may also differ according to whether the transaction that created the security gives the security holder special buffers against financial reverses. One type of credit enhancement is a letter of credit. The security holders, for example, bondholders, may be entitled to require a bank issuing a letter of credit to pay off the bonds in the event that the issuing company fails to do so. Or, the transaction may create a special reserve fund to pay off security holders. Some transactions have more than one credit enhancement, with the various buffers acting as first, second, or third lines of defense against disaster.

Government/Corporate. Government securities carry the promise of the United States government to pay the security according to its terms. These securities are said to be backed by the "full faith and credit of the United States" and, thus, are considered the safest of all securities. By contrast, corporate securities are only as safe as the corporation or asset backing them. Later Keys will help you learn to distinguish between corporate securities that are backed only by the general credit of the issuer and those that are backed by specific assets of the issuers.

There are many other ways to categorize securities in addition to the ones included in this Key. Nonetheless, an understanding of the six basic divisions discussed above will help you to organize your review of the more specific Keys that follow. These six categories will also form the basis of a mental checklist to guide you in your evaluation of securities products.

Security as Contract. Stripped to its legal elements, the security is a contract between the company that issued the security and the investor. Why did the parties enter the contract? They each had different motives and goals or benefits they expect to receive from the security contract. To be enforceable, a contract must give each party a legal benefit and impose on each party a legal obligation. Such obligations and benefits constitute the consideration for the contract, the bargained-for value that is the legal basis of the contract.

The issuer may benefit from the issuance of the security in several ways. Some of the benefits of issuing securities may include

1. raising money in the least costly way.
2. raising the issuer's market profile, by demonstrating it can be a player in a given market.
3. allowing employees to have an ownership stake in their efforts.
4. allowing owners of business to take money out of the business without selling the entire business or losing control.
5. increasing company pride or employee morale by introducing an innovative product or driving to successful conclusion a difficult deal.
6. tax savings.
7. ego enhancement.

Let's assume the benefit the issuer wants to achieve is to raise money. The issuer designs the security to raise money in the least costly way using two basic strategies. Either the issuer can sell the holder a part of itself in the form of an equity security, such as common stock, or it can borrow from the holder by issuing some form of debt security, such as a bond or debenture. A host of factors influence the issuer's choice, including

- the availability of cash to service debt
- pretax and after-tax cost of funding
- the impact of the issuance on existing equity or debt security holders
- the likely reception of the issuance of the security by ratings, courts, the SEC, and state regulators

The fundamental obligation incurred by the issuer of

a securities contract is to deliver to its buyer a security that meets the terms of the contract as they have been disclosed to the buyer. As will be discussed in Keys 41–44, the federal securities laws require issuers to disclose all important features of the security to prospective purchasers. The security's failure to fit the prospectus description could expose the issuer to financial penalties or even jail terms.

For the holder, the benefit of the security is as a means of investing money to earn a potentially higher profit than can be earned on alternative investment outlets. The amount of profit that will satisfy the investor, again, depends on many factors such as the relative safety of the security, the investor's risk/reward profile, whether the holder needs to earn the profit over a short, medium, or long-term horizon, the tax situation of the holder, and the costliness of the security as compared to some external benchmark such as the historical value of similar securities.

The basic obligation of the buyer of a security is to pay the purchase price in the amount and within the time period agreed. Unlike the financial benefit received by the seller, which is paid to the seller when the security changes hands, the financial benefit to the buyer is only the *potential* to earn a profit.

Typical Contract Terms. The features within the four corners of the security contract each are separate keys to understanding the way the security works. The presence of some of these features, such as the purchase price and the interest rate yield, make intuitive sense. The issuer's failure to include a description of certain of these basic features would be noticed by almost all would-be purchasers. For example, an investor would notice the issuer's failure to disclose rate of return as readily as a car buyer would probably notice the seller's failure to disclose the car's price. Other features of the security contract attract much less attention but are equally important, such as whether the security is

10

redeemable. As we have seen, buyers of securities depend on sellers to disclose all material terms of the security contract, and the seller's failure to do so may bring trouble from the SEC or a state regulator.

Despite the incentive the disclosure laws give to sellers to tell all (or run the risk of being penalized for their silence), buyers should have a checklist of questions to identify gaps in the seller's disclosure documents. This Key and the Keys that follow should make you more alert to many of these gaps.

3

RISK AND REWARD

A truism of investment in securities is that greater risks should bring greater rewards. Or, looked at another way, the price of your peace of mind is a lower yield on your investment. Because brokers' and analysts' assessments of the relative riskiness of securities amount to predictions of the future performance of the securities, and since no one can predict the future accurately each time, it is important to appreciate at the outset that even those securities pronounced absolutely safe may carry some degree of risk.

There are several different risks that may come with securities ownership. First, there is the risk that you will not earn the profit on your investment you anticipated. There is also the risk that you may lose your investment entirely. As one joke goes, "It's not just the return *on* your investment that counts, it's the return *of* your investment that should worry you."

Many factors should form the decision of how much risk you should bear for the potential reward the security offers. You should consider, among other things, your yearly disposable income and net worth as well as your short-term income needs, such as vacations and home improvements, and longer-term income needs, such as college tuition and retirement income. Consider also whether you are the type of person who can deal with the uncertainty many securities investments bring.

Once you have considered these factors, you may derive what some financial planners call your risk/reward profile. In general, younger people with few family responsibilities might be willing to take on a higher degree of risk in order to have a chance at the capital appreciation such equity investments might bring.

Even mature investors may take some risk to ensure continuation of income.

4

SECURITY DESIGN

We find it useful to think of securities as we do clothes. Like clothes, securities vary in complexity and function. A security can be as simple as the basic black dress or blue suit, or it can be as ornate and embellished as Queen Elizabeth's coronation gown. Regardless of the style or the design of the security, however, to be successful, it has to fit the needs of the buyers. Fit enough buyers' needs, and the security becomes a classic that never goes out of style. Fit only a few buyers' needs, and the security is a one-season hit, a passing fad.

Keys 5, 6, 25, 28–32, and 34 review some of the basic designs used by those who structure securities—those we call *security designers*—and discusses some of the reasons a designer may choose one style over another. We'll look at some of the classics and review a few of the fads.

As an introduction, we will first review the patterns each would-be purchaser should understand.

5

COMMON STOCK—
THE BASIC EQUITY
SECURITY

The Z Corporation needs money. You are the vice president put in charge of the project to raise the money. The money is needed for a project crucial to Z's future—building a new state-of-the-art mainframe computer plant. You and 12 other vice presidents caucus around a mahogany table to brainstorm. You first decide
- how much money the project requires
- how soon the money will be needed
- whether the money will be needed all at once or whether staggered amounts will do
- how much the company can afford to pay to get the money

Someone suggests drawing down on one of Z's existing lines of credit it maintains with its bank. That idea is rejected because the interest on indebtedness under the line of credit is currently too high. Someone else suggests going to the current bank or a new bank and getting a loan at the somewhat lower current market interest rate—but that rate is still higher than Z would like to pay. Besides, banks ordinarily require collateral, and Z does not want to tie up its collateral for the length of time the banks would require.

You suggest that Z might raise the money from the public. It occurs to you that there are only two ways to raise money from the public.

1. You can *borrow* either against the assets or the credit standing of the company by issuing a debt security.

2. You can *sell* a part of the company, in effect making the public a part owner of Z, by issuing an equity security.

All means of using securities to raise money from the public involve issuing derivatives of either an equity or a debt security or some combination of both.

The consensus around the table is to sell a part of the ownership. The vehicle for consummating that transaction is the basic equity security called *common stock.*

Selling a part of the ownership of the business has its advantages. Unlike the case of borrowing, there are no creditors, no due dates, and no late penalties if Z misses a payment date. Plus, unlike a sale of assets, a sale of common stock does not require that you transfer any of Z's hard assets to the new owner. For example, if you sell 20 percent of Z's stock, the stock does not entitle the stockholder to lay claim to certain computers or certain real estate or certain desks. Instead, the stockholder is deemed to own an undivided share of the value of the business; if all Z's assets, both tangible and intangible, are added together and expenses subtracted, a 20 percent stockholder would own 20 percent of the total bottom line value.

The owners of stock in a corporation, unlike the participants in a partnership or sole proprietorship, have little control over the decision as to whether or not they will be paid their proportionate share of the business profits in the form of dividends each year. The decision about whether to pay dividends or to reinvest the profits in the enterprise—as with most other management decisions affecting the corporation—are the domain of the corporation's officers and directors, not its stockholders. Therefore, in the case of common stock, the purchase should be viewed as a vote of confidence in a company's management and financial policies.

The advantages to the purchaser of stock ownership are numerous. One big advantage is that the law will deem the stockholder to be owner but one with limited

16

liability. The stockholder thus has a chance to share in the sometimes spectacular wealth created when a company like Z becomes profitable. On the other hand, if Z gets hit with misfortune such as a billion dollar lawsuit judgment, the stockholder's losses are limited to the value of his or her shares. The stockholder's other assets—home, bank accounts, stock in other companies—are not vulnerable to Z's bad luck.

In recent years, shareholder rights have been better recognized by boards of directors. Shareholders have been more active as a class and have been ready to exercise their rights and their power to influence recalcitrant company boards by challenging board actions in court.

6

PREFERRED STOCK

An issuer can design a class of stock that, like common stock, represents equity ownership in the issuing company but also carries certain privileges. These privileges generally include the right to be paid dividends before the common stockholders are paid and the right to receive a specific amount in the form of dividends each year.

The payment rights of preferred stock rank ahead of common but behind the interests of outside creditors such as bondholders. If in any year the company fails to pay to preferred stockholders their dividend, the obligation to pay out the dividend could accumulate until the next year or the year after—or whenever the company at last found itself able to pay dividends. Preferred stock with this feature is called *cumulative preferred.* In this sense, cumulative preferred stock resembles a debt security such as a bond. The family resemblance between bonds and preferred stock is strong in another way. Preferreds, unless participating (see below), and bonds, unlike uncommon stock, do not participate in the potential for growth in the company's net profits. Just as the bondholder's reward is limited to a fixed amount of interest, the preferred stockholder's reward is limited to the regular dividend.

Preferreds may also carry the feature of participation. Participating preferred stockholders are paid in two ways.

1. They are paid before common stockholders from the available net income to satisfy fixed dividend rights.
2. Then they are paid again, with common stockholders, from the remaining net income.

Not surprisingly, preferreds are often said to act like bonds. That is, the market value of preferreds fluctuates according to general interest rates, company earnings, and market fears. The analogy does not always prove itself in the real world for reasons unknown to the most brilliant quantitative analyst or market psychologist, but nonetheless, the rule of thumb is still used.

Although preferred stockholders are paid only after all bondholders are paid interest and any principal due, preferreds carry key advantages over bonds for corporate investors. For instance, a corporation investing in the preferred stock of another corporation is entitled to exclude 85 percent of all dividends received from its taxable income; there is no exclusion for bond income. As a result, corporate investors have a strong incentive to buy preferreds over similarly priced bonds.

Convertibles are corporate securities, usually preferred shares or bonds, that are exchangeable for a set number of another form of securities at a prestated price.

7

INITIAL PUBLIC OFFERINGS (IPOs)

If XYZ, a private company, wants to sell ownership to the public for the first time, it would make an *initial public offering,* or IPO. The IPO is accomplished by the use of a formal offer to sell and agreement to buy stock called a *subscription.* A buyer subscribes to the purchase of a certain number of shares at a certain price for the period set in the subscription, and the promoter, on behalf of the issuer, offers to sell the shares at that certain price.

To ascertain the number of investors interested in buying a certain design of security, the issuer or its underwriter may contact certain investors, perhaps circling the names of those who express interest in the securities, a procedure known, appropriately enough, as taking circles. Once circles have been taken, the underwriter has a feel for the potential appetite of the public for the security.

IPOs have helped to create some of the most spectacular fortunes in the history of the country. William H. (Bill) Gates, the founder of Microsoft, the software giant, made a fortune when his company's shares went public in March 1986 for $21 per share, making his 11 million shares worth more than $200 million. As the stock price rose in the next few years, Gates became a billionaire in his early thirties and by the turn of the century had become the richest man in the world, worth close to $100 billion.

Retrades. In a retrade of stock, the higher net worth that may be created through the retrade may indirectly translate into more cash for the issuing company. When stock that originally traded for $10 reaches the retrade price of $20, the value of the shares in the company's inventory doubles, and the company's paper net worth increases. The cost of its borrowings decreases, since the company is now, theoretically at least, more creditworthy. The company can probably increase its lines of credit and therefore its cash reserves by borrowing against its new paper wealth, all this because the market auction has judged the company more valuable today than yesterday.

Generally, however, the stock value of an IPO often rises very quickly upon issue and then frequently falls, so individual investors might want to wait until the stock price has stabilized before considering the IPO as investment potential.

8

BUYING AND SELLING

Now that you have some idea of the type of products available in the market and the methodologies used to value those products, you may decide you want to purchase something you don't have or sell something you do have. There are four basic ways to transfer securities through an exchange.

1. buy
2. sell
3. sell short
4. sell short against-the-box

To effect these transfers, you can use one of four kinds of orders.

1. market orders
2. limit orders
3. stop orders
4. stop-limit orders

There are two methods of paying for the transaction.

1. cash
2. margin

Regular Trading. Say that Bob buys 10,000 shares of Z stock at $5 per share paying $50,000 cash. He holds onto the stock long enough to realize a profit and sells the stock. Bob has engaged in an ordinary buy transaction and an ordinary sell transaction.

Selling Short. *Selling short* means Bob is selling stock he does not own. Bob believes that Z stock is now going to fall in price. He would like to sell the stock at $5 per share, but he doesn't own any shares. Taking advantage of an age-old stock market practice, Bob will *sell short*. When investors buy stock on margin, the broker retains custody of the shares and, generally, the right to lend the shares to short sellers. In this case Bob instructs his broker to borrow 10,000 shares and to sell them at $5 per share. Later, if Z stock declines to, say, $4 per share, Bob may decide to cover his short and buy 10,000 shares. Bob then instructs his broker to return the 10,000 shares to the lender, thus making a profit before commission and other expenses of $1 per share on 10,000 shares, or $10,000. A decline of $2 per share would have yielded a profit of $20,000, a $3 decline, a profit of $30,000, and so on.

To avoid cascading downward values precipitated by short selling, selling short is permitted only when the stock is on the uptick, meaning the last trade quote is at a higher price than the previous quote, or a "zero tick," meaning the last two trade quotes are identical.

One caveat: The potential for loss in a short sale is unlimited. Suppose Z Corporation had become the object of a takeover battle, leaping to $10, $15, $20, or more per share. If Bob was caught short and was finally forced to purchase the stock at $20 per share, his loss would have totaled $150,000! By placing a stop-loss order—say, at $7 per share—Bob could have limited his loss to $20,000. Risky business.

Selling Short Against the Box. Rather than obtaining his relatively cheap inventory of Z stock from the markets, Bob, if he already owned Z stock cheaper than the market price, could effect a special kind of short sale, called a "short against the box." Selling short against the box is selling short stock actually owned by the seller but held in safekeeping (called the box). The motive for selling short against the box, which assumes that the securities needed to cover the short sale are borrowed as with any short sale, may be simply that the securities in safekeeping are inaccessible, or that the seller does not wish to disclose ownership. More often than not, however, the motive is to protect a capital gain in the shares that are owned, while deferring the taxes due if the shares were sold and the capital gain had to be reported.

The practice of selling short against the box is not new. It has been around for at least 50 years and was regarded in the 1930s by some as a way for corporate insiders to conceal dealings in the stock of their corporation. One congressman railed vehemently against the mechanics of short selling and against-the-box trading, vowing that he would "not desist until these invidious and thoroughly reprehensible practices" of short selling and selling against the box were abolished. Why the storm? Part of the sentiment against short selling against the box grew out of the perception that these practices enable corporate officers to conceal short sales of their corporation's stock, which, in effect, is betting on their corporation's misfortune.

In today's market the Securities and Exchange Commission regulates insider trading. *Insider trading* refers to transactions in the securities of a publicly traded company executed by a company insider. Although a company insider might theoretically be anyone who knows material financial information about the company before it goes public, in practice, the list of company insiders, whose company stock-trading activity is made public through the press, is normally restricted to a moderate-sized list of company officers and other senior executives. Smart companies usually warn all employees to be careful when they trade. The U.S. Securities and Exchange Commission (SEC) has strict rules in place that dictate when company insiders may execute transactions in their company's securities. All transactions that do not conform to these rules are, in general, prosecutable offenses under U.S. securities law.

Market Orders. A market order instructs the broker to buy or sell the security at the best price available. The market order "Buy ABC stock" means buy at the lowest price the market offers. The order "Sell ABC" means sell at the highest available market price. All exchanges permit trading through this most basic order.

Limit Orders. These are orders to buy or sell a security at a specified price or better. The broker will execute the trade only within the price restriction. For example, a customer puts in a limit order to by ABC Corp. at $40 when the stock is selling for $42. Even if the stock reached $40 and one-eighth, the broker will not execute the trade. In the same way, if the client put in a limit order to sell ABC Corp. at $43 when the price is $41, the trade will not be executed until the stock price hits $43.

Stop Orders. These are orders to a securities broker to buy or sell at the *market price* once the security has traded at a specified price called the *stop price*. A stop order may be a *day order,* a *good-till-canceled order,* or any other form of time-limit order. A stop order to buy, always at a stop price above the current market price, is usually designed to protect a profit or to limit a loss on a short sale.

A stop order to sell, always at a price below the current market price, is usually designed to protect a profit or to limit a loss on a security already purchased at a higher price.

The risk of stop orders is that they may be triggered by temporary market movements or that they may be executed at prices several points higher or lower than the stop price because of market orders placed ahead of them. Also called *stop-loss order.*

Stop-Limit Orders. These are orders to a securities broker with instructions to buy or sell at a specified price or better (called the *stop-limit price*) buy only after a given *stop price* has been reached or passed. It is a combination of a *stop order* and a *limit order.*

For example, an instruction to a broker might be "Buy 200 ABC Corp 55 STOP 56 LIMIT," meaning that if the market price reaches $55, the broker enters a limit order to be executed at $56 or a better (lower) price.

A stop-limit order avoids some of the risks of a stop order, which becomes a *market order* when the stop price is reached; like all price-limit orders, however, it carries the risk of missing the market altogether, since the specified limit price or better may never occur.

9

INTERNATIONAL SECURITIES

Although the U.S. securities markets are the largest and most financially influential in the world, there are many other sizeable securities markets in the world that could offer the U.S. investor some opportunities for profitable investment, particularly at times when the U.S. securities markets are not performing as well as certain overseas markets.

In this world of instant information our knowledge of the price of or yield from many foreign securities is as available to a U.S. investor as a U.S. security.

There are four ways to invest abroad, each with advantages and disadvantages.

1. U.S. equity issues that have a strong multinational presence.
2. Foreign stocks that are listed on U.S. exchanges and through American depositary receipts (ADRs).
3. Direct purchase of foreign shares by opening a brokerage account in a foreign country.
4. Mutual Funds specializing in foreign stocks.

Rules and Regulations. Because the regulatory requirements regarding disclosure of company information listed in foreign exchanges are different from the U.S. SEC rules, and different from each other, it may be more difficult for an investor to understand the fundamentals of the company in which the investor may be interested.

Only those companies that began trading through ADRs on U.S. exchanges after 1983 must report required financial information to the Securities and Exchange Commission. Such companies as Toyota and Fuji-Photo Film traded through ADRs prior to 1983 and were grandfathered (granted an exemption), and do not have to submit SEC required financial information.

The International Organization of Securities Commissions has been created by various governments to establish more open and more consistent disclosure rules.

An investor in foreign securities must take into account the possibility of currency fluctuations that can enrich or impoverish the investor even if the foreign security involved does not change in price or yield.

Funds and Exchanges. There are four types of funds that deal in foreign securities.

1. *International Funds.* Also known as overseas funds, they diversify investments throughout other countries. They manage investing in mature, stable countries, as well as fast-growing emerging economies.

2. *Global Funds.* Global funds invest in the United States as well as in foreign countries. Managers adjust their exposure to areas of the world depending on how they think the areas will perform.

3. *Regional Funds.* These funds concentrate on a particular part of the global economy, such as Latin America or Asia.

4. *Country Funds.* These funds allow investors to concentrate on a particular country's economy. These funds are generally closed-end, carry high risk, and are not recommended for novice investors. For certain countries, however, country funds are the only way foreign investment is allowed.

The following is a short list of the largest foreign exchanges in the world:

Argentina	Hong Kong	Norway
Australia	India	Philippines
Austria	Indonesia	Portugal
Belgium	Ireland	Singapore
Brazil	Israel	South Africa
Canada	Italy	Spain
Chile	Japan	Sweden
China	Korea	Switzerland
Denmark	Luxembourg	Taiwan
Finland	Malaysia	Thailand
France	Mexico	Turkey
Germany	Netherlands	United Kingdom
Greece	New Zealand	Venezuela

10

CERTIFICATES/ BOOK ENTRY

A purchase of securities can be evidenced by the delivery of a stock certificate. In the past, the beauty of the stock certificate was a matter of pride for an issuer, and companies issued certificates of sometimes elaborate artistry.

You may choose to have the broker register the security in your name and deliver the certificate to you, or to leave the security in the custody of your broker, in which case it will be insured against theft or loss by the SIPC (Securities Investor Protection Corporation) up to a limit of $500,000.

Increasingly, today, the buyer never receives paper evidence of a transaction, which is instead effected through the book-entry system. This system works by reflecting transfers of stock as deductions from or additions to the investor's brokerage account.

Securities held in the name of a broker or another nominee are known as *securities held in street name*. Since the securities are in the broker's custody, transfer of the shares at the time of sale is easier than if the stock were registered in the customer's name and physical certificates has to be transferred.

A *nominee* is a person or firm, such as a bank official or brokerage house, into whose name securities are transferred by agreement. Securities held in street name, for example, are registered in the name of a broker (nominee) to facilitate transactions, although the customer remains the true owner.

11

VOTING RIGHTS AND POWER

Although a share of common stock typically carries with it the right to vote, only the security contract states exactly what voting rights attach to a particular stock. Generally, the axiom of *one share—one vote* holds true. So, if a shareholder purchases 10 percent of XYZ common, the shareholder would be entitled to cast 10 percent of the votes for a new director or 10 percent of the votes to determine whether to approve or reject a merger proposal.

Voting *rights* do not necessarily equal voting *power.* To see the difference, suppose that at the annual meeting shareholders must vote on a merger proposal. Suppose also that insiders control 80 percent of the company's shares. In this case, investors owning 10 percent of the votes have little real power as long as the insiders vote as a block.

Corporate Bylaws. The amount of voting power an investor has also depends on the percentage of votes needed to carry a proposal. All issues coming before the body of shareholders are not deemed equal. The exact percentage required to pass a given measure is set by the corporate bylaws. A simple 51 percent majority can pass some issues; others require a 67 percent affirmance; still others require unanimity.

Majority Vote. If the bylaws don't specify the percentage required to pass a given issue, state statutory law may fill in the blanks. For example, under New York law a majority vote carries a measure to appoint a new director or remove an old director, but a two-thirds vote, a so-called *super majority* must approve a merger.

It would be a mistake to assume that all the common stock of a given issuer carries identical voting rights. For instance, you may be issued shares having a one-half voting right. This means that for every share you own, you would have a right to cast only 0.5 of a vote on any matter. The New York Stock Exchange, recognizing that a scheme that assigns only a fraction of voting right for a full share puts purchasers of such shares at a disadvantage, now requires member companies that issue stock with diluted voting rights to fully disclose to the prospective holders the diluted nature of the stock.

Supershares. To alter the concentration of voting power, a company can issue shares having disproportionately large voting rights, called *supershares.* If you are an existing shareholder and your company issues one-half voting right shares, then your voting power has increased as a result of the higher concentration of voting rights in the old crowd. If, on the other hand, you are an existing shareholder and your company decides to issue new 3-for-1 supershares, your voting power is diluted because of the resulting increase in voting strength in the new shareholders.

The supershare design enables an unusual concentration of voting power, making it easier for holder of such shares to carry proposals, and providing the supershareholders with greater speed of action and maneuverability.

Classes of Stock. Some publicly traded companies separate their shares into more than one class of common stock, usually designated Class A and Class B. The distinguishing features, set forth in the corporation charter and bylaws, usually give an advantage to the Class A shares in terms of voting power, though dividend and liquidation privileges can also be involved.

12

PREEMPTIVE RIGHTS

The issuer may design the security to give its holder the right of first refusal to buy new shares issued by the company—called a *preemptive right* or *subscription warrant*. Preemptive rights act to protect existing shareholders against potential dilution of the price value and voting strength of their shares.

Existing stockholders are not automatically entitled to preemptive rights. Some states require only that issuers give stockholders preemptive rights if the corporation's charter establishes such rights. Some states also permit holders to waive preemptive rights. The shares of many companies do not carry preemptive rights.

Preemptive rights may not apply to shares issued to satisfy convertible security exchanges or shares to be exchanged for the shares of a merger partner.

13

THE ROLE OF UNDERWRITERS

Underwriting is a term that includes a diverse number of undertakings assumed by companies called "underwriters" in connection with making securities available to the investing public. An underwriter performs the function of a middleman, purchasing the securities of an issuing company in bulk and reselling them through its distribution channels to the investing public. The profit the underwriter makes in this type of transaction is the difference between the price it pays for the securities and the price at which it sells them to the public, minus any fees and other expenses. Their ability to distribute securities makes underwriters attractive to an issuing company, which typically lacks the broad selling network of dealers and brokers often needed to reach retail and institutional investors across the country.

An underwriter that has committed itself to purchase an issuance of securities may decide, for financial reasons, to allow other companies to share in the underwriting costs and potential profit. Typically, the company that takes the lion's share of the risk is the lead underwriter, while the other participants are said to form part of the underwriting group. According to the underwriting agreements, the underwriter may be responsible for stabilizing the price of the issuer's shares in the market for a certain period of time, and may be required to bid for these shares (called *pegging*) so that the price does not fall below a specified level.

Underwriters cannot sell or offer to sell the securities until a registration statement has been filed with the

Securities and Exchange Commission (SEC; see Key 37) and has become effective. Before the registration becomes effective, however, underwriters frequently try to obtain preliminary indications of interest from potential customers. Often, the underwriter will try to line up more than enough buyers so that the securities can be sold in a matter of days, or even seconds, after the registration statement becomes effective. An underwriter that comes to market with less than 100 percent of the securities sold faces the risk that the market value of the securities will fall below what the underwriter paid the issuer. Underwriters' fees can be extremely high, as can accompanying attorneys' fees and printing and related costs.

Underwriters can incur liability to investors under a number of theories, including making false or misleading statements in the prospectus that describes the securities.

An investment banking firm can act as an underwriter that serves as intermediary between an issuer of securities and the investing public. In what is termed firm commitment underwriting, the investment banker, either as manager or participating member of an investment banking syndicate, makes outright purchases of new securities from the issuer and distributes them to dealers and investors, profiting on the spread between the purchase price and the selling (public offering) price.

A *syndicate* is an association of investment bankers that, operating under the agreement among underwriters, agrees to purchase a new issue of securities from the issuer for resale to the investment public.

14

GROWTH AND MOMENTUM INVESTING

A stock of a corporation that has exhibited faster-than-average improvement in earnings over a number of years and is expected to continue to have high levels of growth in profit is considered to be a *growth stock*. Over an extended period of time, growth stocks tend to out-perform slower-growth or stagnant stocks. If it is a true growth stock, its earnings will compound at 15 percent or more, no matter what the overall economy is doing.

The easiest way for most people to make money in stocks over the long term is to buy and hold shares in high-quality growth companies. Growth stocks can perform so well because growth stock companies usually offer special, well known, or niche products that have well-known brand names, are financially strong, and have top-performing management. As long as these factors don't change, growth can usually continue indefinitely; however, at some point in their growth, these companies become very large, and for some it becomes more difficult to generate the same level of profit increases.

Growth stocks are riskier investments than average stocks, but they usually have higher price/earnings ratios and frequently are stock from companies that make little or no dividend payments to shareholders. As long as earnings growth continues, there is usually no problem; however, should a growth company report a slight reduction in its earnings growth, or exhibit some other less than sterling performance, the stock can drop precipitously out of all proportion to the small size of the problem. One of the last investments anyone wants to own is a growth stock about to disappoint investors' expectations. A growth stock is sometimes known as a *momentum stock.*

15

EVALUATING SECURITIES

Investing in the stock market, according to some authorities, is a simple matter: All you have to do is buy a stock when its price is too low (undervalued) and sell when the price is too high (overvalued)—and at the race track all you have to do is bet on the horse that wins!

How do you know when a security is trading at a low or a high? The next few Keys explain the art and science of securities valuation. It's important to identify what strategy of investing you are comfortable with, whether you do your investing directly or through an adviser. Though the variety of methods used to value equity securities seems to increase as fast as the variety of securities themselves, it is still possible to identify four basic strategies that have dominated stock analysis for years. The strategies are

1. fundamental analysis
2. technical analysis
3. "new investment analysis"
4. the random walk (*Efficient Market Theory*)

16

FUNDAMENTAL ANALYSIS

We think the best way to understand the differences between the strategies is to begin on Christmas Eve. It's the time of night that has no name, somewhere after the time Santa should have visited but long before the time when you can burst into the living room and open the packages. This Christmas you know you're going to get a *Western Flyer* bicycle because you've spied it in its unglamorous, unassembled state in the attic. As you lie in bed, listening to the voices in the living room, you begin to realize there's a problem. Something is wrong with the assembly of the bike. The world is not right.

Your father is one of those dads who believes he can figure out anything. When the TV broke, he didn't shake or smash it or wait till it came around on its own; he calmly opened the owner's manual, ignored the back panel warning "Do Not Open," and figured out what was wrong. So, it's only natural that in assembling your bicycle he knows he can *make* it work. He opens the trusty owner's manual and begins to read. Hours later, he's still at work, jotting down some calculations, using a ruler to measure carefully, maybe writing on graph paper. This bike will work, he believes, because reason works—reason is provable truth. He is, at his core, a fundamental analyst. And when he reaches a problem that won't obey the laws of reason he assumes he just hasn't reasoned enough.

The fundamental analyst reasons that every stock has a certain, discoverable intrinsic value. If one can ascertain that value, then the decision whether to buy or sell is easy. Buy if the price is lower than that value; sell if the price is higher than that intrinsic value.

Buying a stock is in many ways like buying a company. Because, after all, that's what you're doing as investor, even if you take a flyer or just a few shares. Perhaps, then, it will be useful to look at a sophisticated businessperson in the process of buying an entire company.

Example:

Company ABC is up for sale. Ms. Wise and Mr. Young are considering whether to buy ABC. They, their accountant, and their lawyer review ABC's balance sheets and income statements for each of the past five years and discover that in each of those years ABC has produced about $1 million in after-tax earnings. How much should they pay for ABC?

Determining the appropriate multiple of earnings is an imprecise process, and the ultimate figure paid will represent a compromise between the buyer and seller of the company, the age-old tug of supply and demand. The potential buyers of ABC must consider the following questions:

1. Will ABC continue to earn at least $1 million per year in the future?
2. What kind of multiples do other healthy businesses similar to ABC sell for? Is the average multiple of earnings lower or higher than the one you are offering?
3. What is the return you can earn on alternative investments? Is it less or more than the projected income stream ABC offers? Are the degrees of safety offered by the alternatives comparable to those offered by ABC?

The multiple they decide to pay thus not only represents the arithmetic result of dividing price by earnings but also reflects other aspects of the above analyses.

The P/E ratio is a comparison of stock value and company earnings that helps value the company. There are many other elements of data, such as debt, company assets, sales, cash flow, management, and so on, which the fundamental analyst will examine in order to predict future trends of a company's prospects for success or failure. By appraising a company's prospects, fundamental analysts determine whether a particular stock or group of stocks is *undervalued* or *overvalued* at the current market price.

The most successful investors of all time, including Warren Buffett, Mario Gabelli, and Peter Lynch, have used fundamental analysis in one form or another to make their fortunes.

17

TECHNICAL ANALYSIS

Again, it's Christmas, and there has been a problem getting your bicycle assembled. Only this time your dad believes not so much in reason as in the predictability of basic human nature. Early in December, he opened the box, guessing—correctly in this case—that someone forgot to put in a part. Thus, with bicycle parts in front of him, and having failed in his first attempt to assemble it according to the owner's manual, he snaps his fingers and smiles knowingly. "Isn't that just like human nature," he says. "To sell someone a bike without all the necessary parts." He thus concludes that the only way to come out ahead is to put the unassembled bike back in the box and return it to the store. By pointing out the store's error, he is able to induce them to put the bike together for him.

Thus, the nature of technical analysts is that they invest their mental capital in figuring out the psychology of the faceless herd and the direction that psychology will lead the herd. Then, to make a profit, they bet on the direction of the herd. If an analyst sees that the herd has been feeling prosperous for too long a period, he or she guesses that the herd might soon begin to worry. Anticipating a huge selloff, this analyst sells short.

Technical analysis is the research into the demand and supply for securities and commodities based on trading volume and price studies. Technical analysts use charts and computer programs to recognize price trends in a market, security, or commodity future, which they think will forecast price movements. Most analysis is performed for the short- or intermediate-term outlook for the security in question, but some technical analysts also forecast long-term cycles. Unlike fundamental analysts, technical analysts generally do not concern themselves with the financial condition, such as earnings or strength of the balance sheet, of a company. During the last decade, technical analysts have had, at best, mixed success in predicting market behavior.

Elliott Waves. In the 1980s, the technical analysts and their fabled charts enjoyed a nice spell of popularity, thanks to a chartist named Ralph N. Elliott, whose theories were first published in the early 1930s. Studying charts of stock market movements, Elliott believed he discerned distinct patterns that repeated themselves after roughly five cycles, now called *Elliott waves*. Two Elliott wave theorists of the 1980s, Robert Prechter and A. J. Frost, wrote a book predicting that the 1980s would see a rampaging bull run. Nothing succeeds or convinces like success, and when a bull market of gigantic dimension occurred, appearing to prove the Elliott wave theorists right, the theory and its gurus gained fame and followers.

18

THE RANDOM WALK (EFFICIENT MARKET THEORY)

There are those who believe the nature of the market is the absence in any meaningful sense of predictable behavior. Like the wheel of fortune, the market's behavior is random. They argue that the likelihood of future earnings cannot be predicted from past earnings using fundamental analysis or from market psychology using technical analysis. They believe the tracings of ups and downs, plateaus, and bell curves, are produced by a completely random process. Were you a tiny traveler along a stock earnings curve and someone stopped you on Tuesday and asked "Where will you be on Wednesday?" they believe the true answer the traveler must give is "I don't know, I haven't a clue." In fact, no one has a clue, say the random walkers.

But if the walk is random, is the journey without pleasure for all but the truly aimless and the silly? The complete randomness of the market would be a hard reality to face because, if true, it would mean the market is a pure gamble. Yet, such a gamble involves our pension funds, college endowments, the entire capital structure of the U.S. economy, and the economies of countries all over the globe. The mind rails against the possibility that so much is left to the mathematical indifference of a dice throw.

It has been said that the human brain is incapable of comprehending infinity. It is something like trying to think about nothing. Randomness predicts that certain processes carried out an infinite number of times will produce no meaningful pattern, even though at times pseudo patterns might seem to emerge.

Weak Form of Random Walk. The weak form of the random walk theory is an attack on technical analysis, the theory of securities valuation that attempts to time the swings and cycles of the securities markets, buying in the valleys and selling at the peaks, depending for its success on its ability to predict when a point in time is a valley and when it is a peak.

If you look at a statistically significant amount of data for the securities market, according to the random walkers you will discover that plots and charts of past performance have no meaningful relationship to future performance, that a graph of performance for the last six years, which looks like a sketch of the Manhattan skyline, may very well look like a sketch of the great Plains for the next five years. Lines of market performance are just lines. There is no meaning behind them; no intelligence guides them. You would do as well to dip an ant in ink and let it crawl across a sheet of paper as you would trying to discern meaningful patterns from charts of swings and trends.

The data amassed to discredit technical analysis is formidable and growing, and many feel the theory has been academically discredited.

Strong Form of the Random Walk. The strong form of the random walk theory maintains that neither technical analysis nor fundamental analysis will produce performances any better than a randomly selected portfolio.

We've already dealt with the random walker's criticism of technical analysis. The critique of fundamental analysis is based on the random walker's belief in the complete efficiency of the securities markets. By complete efficiency what is meant is that all information, both from the past and present as well as all information *knowable in the future,* has already been reflected in the market price of a security. Therefore, the theory goes, only the unknown and unknowable—the realm of randomness—are not reflected, putting the fundamental analyst and the random walker on equal footing as predictors.

The random walk theory of efficient markets has become an unpopular theory among many investors and professionals during the last decade. Those who practice fundamental analysis appear to have had better success in the marketplace of the last ten years than technical analysts.

19

VALUE INVESTING

Successful investors, like successful engineers, must have a good understanding of the hard facts expressed in numbers—but then these must be applied properly to real-life cases.

There are many lessons to be learned, and to be a successful investor, learning is essential. Security prices are as volatile as ocean waves; they range from calm to stormy. Shrewd investors must estimate what the possible financial climate is now and is likely to become. They must resist following the crowd.

Value investing, which is a form of fundamental analysis, is one of the best ways to step apart from the crowd and to protect oneself from the unpredictable behavior of the securities markets.

Value investors buy shares in a company as though they were buying the entire company, paying little attention to stock market temperament, the political climate, or other exterior conditions.

As simple as it may sound, value investors buy a stock as if they were buying the corner store. In the process they might ask themselves a series of questions:

- Is the business on sound financial footing?
- Will I be assuming a large debt?
- Does the price include the building and the land?
- Will it generate a steady, strong income stream?
- What kind of return on my investment will it produce?
- Is there potential for sales and income growth?

If the investor comes up with the right answers, and if he or she can buy the store for less than its actual future worth to the buyer, then he or she has found a bargain, and has discovered a value investment.

This is a simplification, of course. The corner store is easier to understand than a global industrial conglomerate such as Unilever, DuPont, or General Motors. However, learning to understand some of the basics of any company, its earning power, its assets, its liabilities, and so on, and therefore its real or intrinsic value, is something that can quickly be learned, no higher math needed.

Benjamin Graham, a famous value investor who made his fortune investing in pre- and post-World War II markets, and who has written many critically acclaimed books on the subject, advises value investors to concern themselves only with those things that matter: "...I have been truly interested solely in such aspects of value as present themselves in a clear and convincing manner, derived from the basic elements of earning power and balance sheet position, with no emphasis at all placed on such matters as small variations in the growth rate from quarter to quarter..."

Today's most famous and successful value investor, Warren Buffett, Chairman of Berkshire Hathaway and third richest man in the United States (in 1999), notes on the virtues of value investing: "It baffles me how many people know of Benjamin Graham but so few follow. We tell our principles freely and write about them extensively in our annual reports. They are easy to learn. They should be easy to follow. But the only thing anyone wants to know is, 'What are we buying today?' Like Graham, we are widely recognized but the least followed."

20

DAY TRADING

Day traders rapidly buy and sell stocks throughout the day in the hope that their stocks will continue climbing or falling in value for the seconds to minutes they own the stock, allowing them to lock in quick profits.

Typically, day traders sit in front of computer screens during the trading day and look for a stock that is either moving up or down in value. They want to ride the momentum of the stock and get out of it before it changes course. They do not know for certain how the stock will move; they are hoping that it will steadily move in one direction, either up or down in value. True day traders do not own any stocks overnight because of the extreme risk that prices will change radically from one day to the next, leading to large losses.

To have a chance for success, day traders should ideally have many years of experience trading on the stock market, have and be familiar with excellent equipment, computers, and so on, and be thoroughly trained in the intricacies of day trading. They should also be disciplined, analytical, patient, calm, and able to deal with heavy losses without panic. They should also have available to them sufficient capital to handle the financial ups and downs of day trading.

Many day trading companies offer facilities, equipment, advice, and training to potential day traders.

Losses. Many day traders frequently buy on borrowed money, hoping they will reap higher profits through leverage, but they also run the risk of higher losses too. Day traders frequently suffer severe financial losses in their first months of trading, and many never graduate to profit-making status.

One company, which offers on-line assistance to day traders, tenders this advice to their members: "Since day trading is considered high risk, we want to remind members that this service is geared for more advanced traders with proper equipment and capitalization. As a general guideline, traders should be using no more than 20 to 30 percent of their liquid assets for trading, in combination with a good mix of traditional investing and fixed income type assets. Additionally, we recommend that members watch the action for several weeks to get a good healthy feel for the markets. New traders to the market should understand that day trading is risky and that we do not want to see anyone lose money."

21

DERIVATIVES, FUTURES, AND OPTIONS

Derivatives. Derivatives are instruments, often leveraged, that are linked to either specific financial instruments or indicators, such as foreign currencies, government bonds, share price indices, or interest rates, or to particular commodities, such as gold, sugar, or coffee, that may be purchased or sold at a future date. Derivatives may also be linked to future exchange, according to contractual arrangement, of one asset for another. The derivative contract itself may be tradeable and have a market value.

Futures. A futures contract is an agreement to buy or sell a specific amount of a commodity or financial instrument at a particular price on a stipulated future date. The price is established between buyer and seller either using the older *open outcry* system, or the newer electronic information and communication technologies. A futures contract obligates the buyer to purchase the underlying commodity and the seller to sell it, unless the contract is sold to another before the settlement date, which may happen if a trader waits to take a profit or cut a loss. This contrasts with options trading, in which the option buyer may choose whether or not to exercise the option by the exercise date.

Options. This is the right to buy or sell property that is granted in exchange for an agreed-upon sum. If the right is not exercised after a specified period, the option expires and the option buyer forfeits the money.

Call Option. A call option gives its buyer the right to buy 100 shares of the underlying security at a fixed price before a specified date in the future—usually three, six, or nine months. For this right, the call option buyer pays the call option seller, called the *writer,* a fee called a *premium,* which is forfeited if the buyer does not exercise the option before the agreed-upon date. A call buyer therefore speculates that the price of the underlying shares will rise within the specified time period. For example, a call option on 100 shares of XYZ stock may grant its buyer the right to buy those shares at $100 apiece anytime in the next three months. To buy that option, the buyer may have to pay a premium of $2 per share, or $200. If at the time of the option contract XYZ is selling for $95 a share, the option buyer will profit if XYZ's stock price rises. If XYZ shoots up to $120 a share in two months, for example, the option buyer can exercise his or her option to buy 100 shares of the stock and then sell the shares for $120 each, keeping the difference as profit (minus the $2 premium per share).

On the other hand, if XYZ drops below $95 and stays there for three months, the call option will expire at the end of that time and the call buyer will receive no return on the $2 a share investment premium of $200.

Put Option. The opposite of a call option is a put option, which gives its buyer the right to sell a specified number of shares of a stock at a particular price within a specified time period. Put buyers expect the price of the underlying stock to fall. Someone who thinks XYZ's stock price will fall might buy a three-month XYZ put for 100 shares at $100 apiece and pay a premium of $2. If XYZ falls to $80 a share, the put buyer can then exercise his or her right to sell 100 XYZ shares at $100. The buyer will first purchase 100 shares at $80 each and then sell them to the put option seller (writer) at $100 each, thereby making a profit of $18 a share.

In practice, most call and put options are rarely exercised. Instead, investors buy and sell options before expiration, trading on the rise and fall of premium prices.

Because an option buyer must put up only a small amount of money (the premium) to control a large amount of stock, options trading provides a great deal of leverage and can prove to be immensely profitable.

Hedging. This is a strategy used to offset investment risk. A *perfect hedge* is one eliminating the possibility of future gain or loss.

A stockholder worried about declining stock prices, for instance, can hedge his or her holdings by buying a put option on the stock or selling a call option. Someone owning 100 shares of XYZ stock, selling at $70 a share, can hedge his or her position by buying a put option giving him or her the right to sell 100 shares at $70 at any time over the next few months. This investor must pay a premium for these rights. If XYZ stock falls during that time, the investor can exercise his or her option, that is, sell the stock at $70, thereby preserving the $70 value of the XYZ holdings. The same XYZ stockholder can also hedge his or her position by selling a call option. In such a transaction, he or she sells the right to buy XYZ at $70 a share for the next few months. In return, the stockholder receives a premium. If XYZ stock falls in price, that premium income will offset to some extent the drop in value of the stock.

In addition to the New York Stock Exchange, and Nasdaq-Amex exchanges, there are a number of stock exchanges that offer futures and options trading, the major ones being Philadelphia Stock Exchange, Chicago Board Options Exchange, Chicago Mercantile Exchange, Coffee, Sugar, and Cocoa Exchange, Inc., New York Cotton Exchange, New York Mercantile Exchange, MidAmerica Commodity Exchange, and Minneapolis Grain Exchange.

Trading in these types of derivatives is not for the faint-hearted or the inexperienced investor. Derivatives have proved to be a risky proposition. Any sudden, unexpected major change in the price of a stock, currency unit, or commodity can totally wipe out an unlucky investor.

22

THE BETA

Most investment strategies can be reduced to the quest for the sure thing. Scratch a fundamental analyst or a technical analyst and you'll find a human being who earns a living by trying to help clients evaluate, or possibly eliminate, risk in their financial portfolios. Implicit in the word *risk* is the quality of unpredictability and thus unmanageability.

Throughout its life, a security carries the basic risk that it will not deliver to its owner as much value as the owner expects.

What are the chances that a security will not live up to expectations? One of the ways academics answer this question is by assessing the security's *beta,* which is a measure of the volatility of a security relative to the market. Securities with betas of "1" are as volatile as the market; other things being equal, they go up and down in price more or less in tandem with the popular stock indexes. Securities with betas of less than 1 are less volatile than the market, and securities with betas greater than 1 are more volatile than the market.

Thus, you should not be surprised if a high beta stock takes a nosedive when the market turns down. You would also expect that investors in a jumpy stock would generally expect to receive higher returns than investors in a less volatile stock. Unfortunately, neither of these predictions has been completely verified by studies of stock performance in actual markets.

Some analysts claim that beta is a measure of risk. This is not true; beta is a measure of volatility.

23

MUTUAL FUNDS AND UNIT INVESTMENT TRUSTS

A mutual fund is operated by an investment company that raises money from shareholders and invests it in stocks, bonds, options, commodities, or money-maker securities. These funds offer investors the advantages of diversification and professional management. For these services they charge a management fee, typically 1 percent to 3 percent of assets per year.

Mutual funds may be invested aggressively or conservatively. They may be concentrated in market segments, such as high-tech securities, or financial securities. Investors should assess their own tolerance for risk before they decide which fund would be appropriate for them.

One thing to remember is that you *don't* own the stock in which the fund invests. For example, suppose you put some money in a mutual fund that invests exclusively in GNMAs, a security that is backed by the full faith and credit of the United States. Is your investment in the fund perfectly safe? No.

Consider another fund that invests exclusively in government securities, Treasury bills, and Treasury bonds. These, again, are backed by the full faith and credit of the United States. If you invest in this fund, is your money perfectly safe? No.

In both of these examples, the investors did not directly buy the safest securities. Instead, they bought shares in a *company that invests in the safest securities*. If such a fund suffers a loss, the shareholders will share in that loss, notwithstanding that the underlying security is protected by the U.S. government. Indeed, the mutual fund is the owner of record of all the securities in its portfolio. In the worst case, if the mutual fund went bankrupt, the investors in the fund would merely be the owners of a bankrupt company, taking their place in line for payment in accordance with the rules of bankruptcy. Fortunately, the performance of mutual funds with respect to bankruptcy risk historically has been excellent.

Unit investment trusts (UITs) are large portfolios of securities divided into shares issued to investors. UITs have fixed portfolios: Once the UIT is established, the securities in the portfolio never change until they mature or are called by the issuer. UITs, in contrast to mutual funds, are not managed, and therefore investors in UITs may save management fees. Units in the trust, which usually cost $1,000, are sold to investors by brokers for a load charge of about 4 percent.

Like mutual funds, UITs offer investors a chance to diversify their holdings. Because the quality of the UIT depends on the quality of the securities in the portfolio, investors should be careful that they understand the composition of the UIT portfolio. The investor should also be wary of how UITs advertise themselves. Mutual funds are subject to new rules prescribing the way in which they may state yields and the content of their advertisements. UITs are not subject to the same regulations.

24

PASS-THROUGH SECURITIES

Just as common stock is an equity security representing partial ownership of the company issuing the stock, a pass-through security represents a fractional ownership in a specific asset or pool of assets. The pass-through security is well named. Under this vehicle, a company, which may also be the seller of the asset, agrees to collect the cash flow generated by the asset and to pass it through to the true owners of the asset, the security holders, in accordance with the terms of the pass-through pooling agreement. The collector of the cash flow is called the *servicer.* In a mortgage-backed pass-through security, for example, the servicer agrees to undertake a number of housekeeping functions such as collecting the mortgage payments and coordinating foreclosure of properties if necessary.

The pass-through equity is an attractive design to issuers. For one thing, if the issuer properly structures the transaction, the issuer will be deemed to have removed the assets from its books. This off-balance sheet treatment of equity pass-through interests can bring tax savings. Moreover, if the issuer is a banking institution, off-balance sheet treatment may reduce the amount of cash reserves the issuer is required to maintain against assets.

Real estate investment trusts (REITs) and real estate mortgage investment conduits (REMICs) are just two examples of pass-through securities.

Most pass-through mortgage securities are issued and/or guaranteed by Ginnie Mae, Fannie Mae, or

Freddie Mac, and carry an implied AAA credit rating. The remainder are privately issued and generally rated AAA or AA. The payments of principal and interest are considered to be secure; however, the cash flow on these investments may vary from month to month, depending on the actual prepayment rate of the underlying mortgage loans.

Pass-through securities can be purchased only from your broker.

25

REITs AND REMICs

REITs. Real estate investment trusts (REITs) were created by Congress in 1960 to give larger numbers of Americans a means of investing in real estate projects that previously were accessible to only the wealthy. To help ensure that REITs involve a large number of investors, Congress requires that REITs maintain a minimum of 100 investors and that no fewer than five investors own 50 percent of the REIT. As of 1999 the 210 REITs traded actively on the New York, American, and Nasdaq stock exchanges had an asset value of $131 billion.

REITs basically are designed to pass through all income from the real estate properties and other assets managed by the REIT to investors. So long as all the income is distributed during the tax year in which it is received, the income is taxed only when it reaches the hands of the investors and not at the entity level. As a result, investors receive income that otherwise would be used to pay taxes. REITs must follow strict tax guidelines to retain their status as REITs. Loss of the REIT status can bring financial penalties from the IRS, making the investment less profitable.

Subject to percentage requirements and limitations on certain of the assets they may own, REITs can derive income from a number of real estate and real estate-related sources including

1. rents from real estate
2. income from foreclosed property
3. mortgages
4. refunds of taxes and abatements on real estate
5. income from the sale or disposition of shares in other REITs

REITs have had a spotty performance as investment vehicles since their introduction. In the 1970s, some industry analysts even pronounced the vehicle terminally ill, although more recently others have maintained that REITs have outperformed common stock for significant periods during their 40-year existence. Because the success of a REIT depends on its management's ability to select potentially profitable assets and to manage them well, investors should scrutinize management's track record as well as the performance of the particular REITs under consideration before making investments in these vehicles.

REMICs. Real estate mortgage investment conduits (REMICs) are creations of the 1986 Tax Code, the result of an intense lobbying effort to remove many of the tax impediments to bringing mortgage-backed securities with different classes of interests (multitranched) to investors. Like REITs, REMICs are pass-through vehicles. Unlike REITs, which can invest in real estate and mortgages, REMICs must invest only in mortgages.

REMICs have two classes of interests, *regular* and *residual.* Although a REMIC may have many classes of regular interests, it may have only one residual class. Regular interests typically are deemed debt interests under the tax code. The residual interests are deemed equity interests and represent the income that remains after payment of all the regular classes. Residual interests can carry astonishingly high rates of interest—sometimes in excess of 1000 percent annually—but they also shoulder most of the risk of prepayment. These products are usually sold in $1 million minimum denominations, and thus are mainly bought by institutional investors.

As discussed earlier in Key 24, one of the main risks investors in certain mortgage-backed securities face is the possibility that the underlying borrowers will prepay the mortgages faster than expected, thereby depriving investors of the interest income they could have earned over a longer repayment schedule. REMICs allow issuers to structure classes of mortgage-backed securities with more certain repayment schedules by dividing the classes of securities backed by the underlying mortgages into tiers, according to how fast each will be paid off. The first tier (called a "tranche" in the industry) is entitled to be retired by the underlying mortgage principal and interest first, the second tranche next fastest, the third tranche a bit slower, and so on. The fast pay/slow pay multitranched structure allows the issuer to shift the risk of prepayment to the slower tranches. Investors in the slower tranches thus accept greater prepayment risk, and buy the security on that basis.

26

U.S. GOVERNMENT AND QUASI-GOVERNMENT PASS-THROUGHS AND PAY-DOWNS

Ginnie Maes, Fannie Maes, Freddie Macs—what each of these homespun acronyms have in common is that each refers to securities that are, or are perceived to be, guaranteed by the U.S. government, acting directly or through one of its agencies. Securities thus guaranteed are backed by the full faith and credit of the United States, a magical blessing that means the security holder can sleep easy at night, secure in the knowledge that if the issuer won't pay or can't pay, Uncle Sam will.

Ginnie Maes. Ginnie Maes are securities guaranteed by the Government National Mortgage Association (GNMA), commonly known as Ginnie Mae. GNMA is wholly owned and operated by the U.S. Department of Housing and Urban Development (HUD), whose secretary is a member of the president's cabinet.

In 1970 GNMA issued the first public mortgage-backed pass-through security. GNMA pass-throughs are technically issued by private companies but carry the GNMA guarantee. Only mortgages issued by the Veterans Administration (VA) or the Federal Housing Administration (FHA) may be used in GNMA-guaranteed pools. GNMA guarantees investors in its securities the timely payment of both principal and interest.

Each month investors receive the principal and interest from mortgages in the GNMA pool in which they invest, minus a fee to the lender for servicing the mortgage payments. Thus, payments on Ginnie Maes include both interest *and* return of principal. The latter can represent a trap for unsophisticated investors.

Suppose the mortgages in a particular GNMA pool have an average interest rate of 11 percent. What happens if interest rates fall to 7 percent? Many mortgagees will decide to refinance, obtaining a new mortgage at a lower rate and paying off the old mortgage. As the old 11 percent mortgages drop out of the GNMA pool, the outstanding principal balances are funneled through to the investors in a lump-sum prepayment. This can be bad news for investors. Rather than receiving, say, $500 a month for the next 15 years, the investors may receive a lump sum paying off most or all of their investment and thus denying them the interest they thought was guaranteed. Such investors will probably lose money on the deal because the alternative investment opportunities available to the GNMA investor will pay a lower rate.

The risk of prepayment is a basic wild card of mortgage-backed or, for that matter, any asset-backed securities. Many of the important early innovations in mortgage-backed securities were motivated by a desire to eliminate or mitigate the risk to investors that prepayments will be dumped in their laps. Today's major investment banking houses are teeming with quantitative whizzes (called *quants*) who are in constant quest of the perfect mathematical prepayment model that will bring a good measure of long-term stability to the over $1.7 trillion market in mortgage-backed securities. Before the quants began their quest for the perfect prepayment model, most market participants used a standard prepayment model that assumed a constant prepayment rate (the "CPR" model) over a 12-year period. However, because the CPR predicts an even level of prepayments over a 12-year period, its calculations often bear little resemblance to the roller-coaster swings of interest rates in the real world.

Fannie Maes. Originally chartered in 1968, the Federal National Mortgage Association (FNMA, or Fannie Mae) is a private corporation chartered by the U.S. government. Fannie Mae's stock is traded on the New York Stock Exchange. FNMA securities are not supported by the full faith and credit of the United States. They are only backed by the corporate guarantee of FNMA, though many in the market for government securities do not price FNMAs to reflect a lower credit-worthiness than GNMAs because they believe that the federal government would bail out FNMA if the association got into financial trouble. Fannie Maes are subject to the same prepayment risks as Ginnie Maes, and FNMA, like GNMA, guarantees the timely payment of both principal and interest.

Freddie Macs. Freddie Macs are securities backed by pools of mortgages issued by the Federal Home Loan Mortgage Corporation (FHLMC or Freddie Mac) and carrying Freddie Mac's guarantee of timely payment of principal and ultimate payment of interest.

In 1983 Freddie Mac issued the first public CMO (collateralized mortgage obligation). The designers of the CMO fashioned the instrument to solve the puzzle of prepayment risk. The CMO softens and, in some cases, eliminates prepayment risk. The CMO structure can be understood as a combination of two structures treated in Keys dealing with the pass-through equity security (Key 24) and the bond (Key 29). Like the bond, the CMO is a debt secured by certain collateral pledged by the issuer. In the case of the CMO, however, the income stream from the collateral performs actively to pay down the IOU. This pay-down feature of the CMO resembles the structure of the familiar industrial revenue bonds, which are paid by revenues generated from specific projects such as gas and electric utilities. Contrast the active performance of the CMO collateral income stream with the passive traditional pledge that is used to pay down bond debt only if the corporate issuer first defaults on the

IOU. In the passive pledge case, the collateral is reached by the bond creditor only in a worst-case scenario. In the active pledge, pay-down case, the cash stream from the collateral is expected to be consumed by the IOUs. In that the money from the assets flows through to meet the contractual payments under the security, the CMO is like the pass-through.

Privately issued CMOs do carry some risk. These CMOs rely on the sole obligation of their issuer and are not guaranteed by any government entity.

27

SPECIAL TYPES OF ISSUERS

A corporation can issue securities in its own right or it can create special issuing vehicles. Two of the major issuing vehicles are *special or limited purpose* corporations and *grantor trusts*.

Special-Purpose Corporations. Rather than issuing securities in their own name, corporations sometimes set up special entities to issue the securities in order to get a better rating or to get favorable tax, accounting, or regulatory treatment for the securities. To qualify for special treatment, these special companies must be set up to operate independently of the control of the corporation. For example, the vehicle typically has its own accounts separate from the corporation's accounts, its own officers and directors, and its own shareholders. Typically, these special-purpose corporations or special-purpose vehicles (SPC or SPV) are entities established by a company to raise money from investors by taking advantage of a cash-flowing asset of the company, such as mortgages or accounts receivable. For example, a corporation may sell its best mortgage receivables to the SPC, thereby gaining cash. The SPC could then issue a security collateralized by the mortgage receivables to the public. The SPC charter ordinarily forbids the SPC from acquiring any obligations other than those related to the security.

The beauty of this arrangement is that the SPC, thus insulated, could actually achieve a higher credit rating than the founding corporation, which has many creditors with both unsecured and secured claims against it, while the SPC has only the security holders as creditors, and the mortgage receivables fully secure their claims. In addition, the assets of the corporation may vary in quality, and contracts dealing with those assets may be subject to *cross-defaults* (if the corporation defaults on one contract, other contracts to which the corporation is a party may automatically go into default). As a result, Z Corporation ultimately may have to pay less, in terms of yield to the public, to raise the same amount of money using an SPC than it would have to pay if it issued the security in its own right.

Grantor Trusts. The grantor trust is a tax structure used to hold assets in an arrangement that minimizes income tax liability. Current tax regulations require that the pool of assets such as mortgages or automobile receivables placed in the grantor trust remain fixed and that the interest of holders in the trust not be altered through reinvestment or substitution or alteration of assets in the pool.

In exchange for obeying these constraints, the profits of the grantor trust will be taxed only once (in the hands of the investors), unlike the profits of a corporation, which are taxed twice—once at the corporate level and again when individual holders pay taxes on their dividends.

The security issued by the grantor trust typically represents a slice of the ownership of the underlying mortgages or other receivables in the trust. Of course, as an owner of the mortgage, the investor faces the risk that the underlying borrowers will default on their mortgage payments. The investor also faces the risk that the underlying borrowers will decide to prepay their mortgages, depriving investors of the interest-rich cash flow stream they counted on in buying the receivables.

28

DEBT SECURITIES: AN OVERVIEW

All debt securities represent the issuing corporation's promise to pay. The debenture is the issuer's (unsecured) promise—an IOU—to repay the debenture holder according to the terms of the debenture.

You may recall from Key 2 that debt securities can be classified as either *unsecured* or *secured.* A security is said to be unsecured if the corporation's promise to repay the IOU is backed only by the corporation's willingness and ability to pay, that is, its general creditworthiness. A security is secured if it is backed by a pledge of specific collateral, such as real estate or equipment. In effect the issuer is saying to the investor, "If I don't repay, you can have title to my pledged asset."

Even so, an unsecured debenture still offers a claim against a defaulting corporation senior to that of a stockholder.

The distinction between unsecured debt and secured debt is critical in the event of the bankruptcy of the issuer. In bankruptcy cases, secured investors have claims against specific pledged assets; unsecured creditors, however, are paid off out of any remaining general assets of the issuer. As a result, unsecured creditors may receive only a small fraction of each dollar of their claims.

As with any loan, the terms of the debenture reflect the expectations of both parties. The principal amount of the loan, the interest, the deadline for repaying the loan, and late-payment penalties all are typical debenture terms.

In deciding whether to purchase the debenture, the prospective investor should conduct an analysis almost identical to that made by a bank loan officer. That is, the debenture holder should evaluate the likelihood that the issuing corporation will repay its IOU.

The factors the investor should weigh in making this evaluation include (1) whether the corporation has a history of paying its debts on time (its credit rating), (2) the overall financial health of the corporation, and (3) any other indications, intangible or tangible, of the willingness and ability of the corporation to repay its debt. In addition to the prospectus and annual reports, this information can be obtained from several sources (see Key 37).

The investor should also decide whether the amount of interest the corporation is willing to pay would offer adequate compensation when compared with alternative investments. Unlike a bank making a loan, the debenture holder is not entirely free to negotiate the interest rate compensation for the risk of nonpayment. Why? By the time debentures are offered to most would-be purchasers, their price has been set by the marketplace, presenting the investor with a take-it-or-leave-it decision.

From the point of view of the issuing corporation, the decision to issue debentures will have been made after reviewing the cost of borrowing in the marketplace. Another factor that may heavily influence the issuer's decision to issue debt securities, such as debentures or bonds, to the public rather than to obtain a loan from its banker is personal liability. That is, for multimillion-dollar loans many bankers would require the head of a private company to personally guarantee the large loan. By contrast, an issuance of securities to the public typically does not involve such a guarantee. And given a choice between putting their necks personally on the line for millions in debt or paying extra interest points to investors in a securities issuance, many executives opt to have their companies pay the extra cost to issue to the public. The cost of the money to the borrower will depend on the size of the borrowing and, again, the creditworthiness of the corporation.

If the debt security is issued to the public, it must be issued pursuant to an indenture that provides for the appointment of a trustee to act on behalf of the debt security holders. Certain basic terms of the indenture are set by federal law, such as the requirement that the trustee be independent of the issuer and act to protect the interests of bondholders.

29

BASICS ON BONDS

Today's U.S. bond market represents more than $11 trillion in outstanding debt obligations and is by far the world's largest securities market, larger even than the U.S. stock market. Just over one third of this debt is issued by the U.S. government.

Like the debenture, the corporate bond is an issuer's IOU. But the bond IOU is collateralized by specific assets of the company, which may be seized by the bondholder's representative (ordinarily a trustee) if the company fails to make principal or interest payments when due.

Maturities. Maturity refers to the date on which the security contract calls for the borrower, or issuer, to pay back the investor's initial investment. Often the terms for a bond allow for a call or redemption date earlier than maturity, at the option of the issuer. It's important for investors to know the details of any such options.

Debt securities such as debentures or bonds vary in length of maturity, ranging from two weeks to several decades. If the maturity is three months (such products are sometimes called bills), for example, the security holders can expect to be paid back at the end of the three-month period, unless the issuer defaults on its IOU to the security holder.

For more complex securities such as a collateralized mortgage obligation (CMO), discussed more fully in Key 26, the concept of maturity works in the same way. The security holder, called a noteholder, contracts to lend money to the debtor/issuer in exchange for the receipt of yield-profit at a certain point in time, which is the maturity of the CMO security. Moreover, early redemption ordinarily is penalized by loss of yield-profit in the case of the noteholder or payment of interest penalties in the case of the issuer.

Discount or Interest-Bearing. A debt security can be purchased for a percentage of its par face value, a so-called *discount security.* For example, the security with a face value of $10,000 may sell for $9,800, paying $10,000 at maturity.

In contrast to discounts, interest-bearing debt securities are purchased at par and provide that the purchaser will receive a certain amount of interest over the term of the security, payable typically in monthly or quarterly installments.

High Yield. These are lower-quality bonds that carry more risk, offer higher yield, and are frequently used as vehicles to raise money in mergers and takeovers. These are often known as *junk bonds.*

Investment Grade. These are high-quality investment grade bonds that offer lower yield but carry lower risk. These bonds are more suitable for individual investors.

For specific rating system see Key 35.

Coverage. The bondholder, as a creditor to the company, is concerned with the likelihood that the company will pay the interest due on the IOU in a timely manner and will ultimately pay the IOU's principal. One of the chief measures of that likelihood is the "coverage," defined as the number of times earnings of a company will cover the debt service represented by the bonds for a given period. The basic formula for coverage is as follows:

$$\text{Net income/debt service} = \text{coverage}$$

What category of interest expense ends up in the denominator varies with the authority you consult. For example, you might select as a measure of safety the relationship the total debt incurred by the company bears to the total amount of pretax earnings of the company over the past 7 years. The resulting coverage would be a rough estimate of the company's creditworthiness.

30

FIXED-INCOME AND VARIABLE-INCOME SECURITIES

The phrase *fixed income* refers to a security that can be expected to pay the investor a certain total amount of yield-profit, usually in equal installments, over the term of the investment. The rate of return on a fixed-income investment is thus set at a given level. Both corporate and government bonds and preferred stock are usually called *fixed-income securities* because most of them pay fixed interest or dividends. For this reason, many investors who value knowing how much money their investments will bring in order to plan their budgets, such as the newly retired or elderly or conservative investors, often include fixed-income securities in their portfolios.

The basic risk in holding fixed-income securities is inflation. As inflation rises, the purchasing power of the real yield-profit on a fixed-income investment will drop, and thus the value of the security could decline. As a result, the holder of the fixed-income security would not be able to sell his or her security for the amount he or she paid for it.

The term *variable income security* refers to securities with rates of return that vary according to an agreed-upon index. For these securities, the volatility of interest rates in the upward direction is good news. In the downward direction, the news may be bad or good depending upon what index is used. For example, a security might provide for an initial rate of 7 percent with increases or decreases in the rate of return indexed to the rate of inflation with the proviso that the rate will never fall below 3 percent. Thus, the security holder has some protection against increases in the cost of living, and if there is deflation, his or her rate would never fall below 3 percent.

The Index. Indices are used with preferred stock, mortgage-backed securities, bonds, and other securities designed to allow the rate paid to the investor to float in relation to an external measure. Below is a list of indices commonly used for floating rate securities.

1. *Eleventh District Cost-of-Funds.* The Federal Home Loan Bank System is divided into districts. The Eleventh District publishes an index— expressed as a rate per annum—of bank cost-of-funds through the Federal Home Loan Bank Board of San Francisco. Lenders are attracted to this index because it helps them to pass along the cost of funds they use, to make mortgages and other loans, to the consumer, thereby avoiding a mismatch of assets and liabilities.

2. *One-Year Treasury Securities.* This rate, also expressed per annum, is equal to the weekly average of the closing market bid yields of actively traded United States Treasury securities adjusted to a constant maturity of one year. This rate is published by the Board of Governors of the Federal Reserve System in Statistical Release No. H.15.

3. *LIBOR.* The London Interbank Offered Rate, which is the rate the most creditworthy banks in Europe charge each other for loans over a certain size.

4. *Prime Rate.* The rate banks in the United States charge their most creditworthy customers. The prime rate varies from bank to bank, although most banks tend to keep their rates more or less identical with those of their competitors.

Interest-Rate Sensitivity. A security is said to be interest-rate-sensitive if its value moves up or down with movements in interest rates. Bonds, for example, are said to be interest-rate-sensitive. A bond bought for $1,000 yielding 10 percent will drop in value if interest rates rise, and increase in value if interest rates fall. How much the decrease or increase will be depends on the date of maturity—when the holders receive the $1,000 face value from the issuer. The closer the bond is to its maturity, the closer it gets to its face value.

The designer of the bond can make the security less sensitive to interest rate swings in a number of ways. For instance, the bond interest rate could be tied to some external index of general interest rate movement. Then, whenever interest rates moved up, the value of the bond would make a positive adjustment. Bond value could be further protected by providing in the security contract that the index would only work in the upswing direction. That is, if interest rates moved *down,* the index would move slowly on the downside or remain stable at a given preset floor rate.

31

ZEROS AND CONVERTIBLES

A zero-coupon bond is a security that makes no periodic interest payments but instead is sold at a deep discount from its face value. The buyer of such a bond receives the rate of return by the gradual appreciation of the security, which is redeemed at face value on a specified maturity date.

Some deep-discount bonds pay no interest at all until maturity. These are called, appropriately enough, *zero-coupon bonds*. The IRS has taken the view that, even though the holder receives no interest until maturity, the holder of a zero-coupon bond will nonetheless be taxed annually on the interest accrued.

Convertibility refers to the ability of the holder of the security to exchange it for another security, usually debt exchanged for equity. Therefore, a zero-coupon bond is the issuer's IOU for which the purchaser pays less than face value and receives face value at maturity.

Assume you have a $60,000 face value five-year zero-coupon convertible bond that you bought at discount for $50,000. At the end of five years, you elect to exercise your right to trade in the bond for a common stock equivalent. The term of the bond states that you may trade in the bond for an equivalent number of common shares at a price of $50 per share. Thus, you will receive

$50,000/$50 per share = 1,000 shares of stock

The bond could have fixed the number of shares rather than the price. For example, the bond could have given you an election to cash in the bond for 1,200 shares at maturity, in which case your per share cost is

$$\$50,000/1,200 \text{ shares} = \$41.67$$

If the market price of the share is above $41.67 (plus commissions and other execution costs), you make an immediate profit by electing to convert. But be aware that, depending on the ratio at which you may exchange debt for equity, the conversion may put you in a position of paying more for the equity shares than you would pay if you simply went into the market and made a purchase.

Notice that the issuing company may design the zero-coupon convertible bond in a way to limit or even eliminate its cash outlay.

You can find a number of zero-coupon convertible bonds through the brokerage houses. For example, Liquid Yield Option Notes or LYONS are Merrill Lynch's proprietary version of a zero-coupon convertible bond. LYONS have a put option three years into a 20-year issue.

32

U.S. GOVERNMENT SECURITIES

Three types of government securities dominate the market today—Treasury bills (called T-bills), Treasury notes, and Treasury bonds.

Each of these government securities represents the U.S. government's IOU, backed by the full faith and credit of the United States. The only risk the investor faces is that the government will default, a risk the market has deemed to be zero. For this reason, you often hear government securities described as the safest securities available.

Since safety usually is acquired as a tradeoff to yield, the interest rate on government securities, as set by the auction process described below, traditionally lags behind corporate bonds of the same principal amount and maturity.

The Auction Process. The prices of government securities are set by auction at the branches of the Federal Reserve Bank. How often a government security is auctioned depends on its type. For example, three- and six-month T-bills are auctioned each Monday, while one-year T-bills are auctioned monthly, usually during the first two weeks of the month. To find out when an auction is to take place, you can call either the nearest Federal Reserve Bank directly or a bank or investment house near you that places orders for individual investors with the Federal Reserve Bank. You can e-mail the Treasury (see e-mail address below). To place an order for a Monday auction of a three-month T-bill, the customer must call by Friday. If you buy directly from the Federal Reserve, you are not charged any fee.

A number of on-line brokerages (see Key 40, On-line Investment Resources) will take orders for government securities. You can also buy them directly from the Treasury Department by using their web site

(*www.publicdebt.treas.gov*)

or going to *TreasuryDirect* and placing your order on-line or calling them at 800-943-6864.

You can e-mail the Treasury Department with any questions you may have about their products or services at the following addresses.

Auctions and Results	*AUCTIONS@bpd.treas.gov*
U.S. Savings Bonds	*savbonds@bpd.treas.gov*
Government	
Securities Act	*GOVSECREG@bpd.treas.gov*
The Public Debt	*OPDA@bpd.treas.gov*
Inflation-Indexed	
Securities	*AUCTIONS@bpd.treas.gov*
Procurement	*Procurement@bpd.treas.gov*
State and Local Government	
Securities	*OSAS-DSI@bpd.treas.gov*
T-Bills, Notes,	
and Bonds	*OSAS-DCS@bpd.gov*
TreasuryDirect	
Customers	*OSAS-DCS@bpd.gov*

How Do Treasury Bills, Bonds, and Notes Differ? Although T-bills, Treasury notes, and Treasury bonds are all debt securities, they differ in the length of their maturities. T-bills have the shortest maturities of the three; Treasury notes are intermediate-term securities; and Treasury bonds have the longest maturity. The products also differ in the minimum amount of money you must invest to purchase them. The table on page 80 summarizes how the features of bills, notes, and bonds differ.

Series EE, HH/H, and Series I Savings Bonds. A Series EE bond is an accrual type security (interest is paid when the bond is cashed). The interest rate on EE bonds is calculated as 90 percent of six-month averages of five-year Treasury Marketable Securities yields. EE bonds are sold at 50 percent of the face value of the bond. EE bonds earn interest for up to 30 years.

A Series I bond differs from the Series EE bond as follows: Earnings on I bonds are inflation-indexed. The earnings rate is calculated as a combination of a fixed-rate of return and a semiannual inflation rate based on CPI-U (Consumer Price Index). I bonds are sold at face value.

Series HH/H bonds are current-income securities. This means that, unlike the series EE bond, the HH bond doesn't increase in value. When an HH bond is issued, you pay the face amount. Interest payments are made every six months, providing current income. Series HH bonds pay interest at a fixed rate set on the day you buy the bond. The current rate of 4 percent has been in effect since March 1, 1993. Interest rates are reset on the tenth anniversary of the HH bond's issue date.

You can't buy HH bonds for cash. You can get them only in exchange for Series EE bonds and savings notes or upon reinvestment of the proceeds of matured Series H bonds.

How to Buy Series EE and Series I Bonds. Series EE and Series I bonds can be bought directly from the Treasury Department as noted above, or on-line (24 hours a day) at *http://www.savingsbond.gov.,* using a Visa or MasterCharge credit card at the Savings Bond Connection. You can also authorize the government to deduct the cost of the bonds directly from your bank account. This is known as the Easy Saver program.

T-BILLS

Maturity	Minimum Investment	Increment	Auction Held
3 months	$10,000	$1,000	each Monday
6 months	10,000	1,000	each Monday
1 year	10,000	1,000	monthly

T-NOTES

Maturity	Minimum Investment	Increment	Auction Held
2 years	$5,000	$5,000	monthly
3 years	5,000	5,000	quarterly
4 years–10 years	1,000	1,000	quarterly

T-BONDS

Maturity	Minimum Investment	Auction Held
Over 10–30 years	$1,000	quarterly

33

CREDIT ENHANCEMENTS

As mentioned, bonds and debentures are the issuer's IOUs. Debentures are IOUs backed only by the promise of the debtor/issuer to repay, while bonds are IOUs secured by collateral of the debtor/issuer. To allay investors' fears about the safety of the principal amount of the IOU, the issuer can use *credit enhancements* or *credit supports* such as letters of credit issued by a bank in favor of the security holder, reserve funds, or senior/subordinated structures.

The Letter of Credit. The letter of credit (LOC) is an undertaking by a bank to pay a beneficiary designated by its customer if certain conditions are met. Specifically, the LOC is a letter to a bank from one of its customers asking the bank to agree to pay a third party a specified amount under certain conditions. Suppose, for example, that you plan to buy securities from Z Corporation. To add value to its securities, Z obtains an LOC from its bank in favor of you, the investor. The terms of the LOC call for the bank to pay you if Z fails to meet its obligations under the security. The LOC thus acts as a credit enhancement to securities issued by Z to you and other investors.

In exchange for its promise to honor the LOC according to its terms, the bank receives a fee from Z for establishing the LOC. The bank can be sued by the investors if it fails to pay the LOC according to its terms.

LOCs fall into two categories: direct and standby. The direct LOC may be drawn on by the person for whose benefit the LOC was established immediately upon the maturation of the security. The beneficiary need not ask the issuer to meet its underlying obligations first before drawing on the LOC.

An irrevocable standby LOC is used in lieu of other financial assurances, bond, etc., and may be drawn on by the beneficiary if the issuer fails to provide alternate financial backing during the time period specified in the LOC.

34

SENIOR/SUBORDINATED STRUCTURES

An increasingly common form of credit enhancement is a subordinated interest issued by the company at the same time as the bond or other IOU. For example, if Z Corporation wishes to raise money from the public, Z Corporation can set aside a pool of mortgages or other receivables and design two securities backed by the pool, a 90 percent senior interest and a 10 percent junior interest. The senior security entitles its holder to receive 90 percent of the cash flow produced by the mortgages, after administrative fees, and the junior security holders receive the remaining 10 percent of the cash flow.

As long as all homeowners make their mortgage payments on time and in full, the senior holder would receive $.90 for every dollar of a mortgage payment, and the junior holder would receive $.10 of every dollar. If something happens to interrupt the cash flow from the mortgages, the senior 90 percent holders receive the cash flow that would otherwise go to the 10 percent junior holder. As a result, for any month in which the underlying homeowners fail to pay their mortgages, the senior holder is buffered against cash flow interruption.

This 10 percent buffer enhances the value of the senior securities, but issuers sometimes find it difficult to sell the junior securities. As a result, many issuers retain the junior interest, if the price and tax benefits of issuing the senior are greater than the costs of retaining the junior. If the junior securities are sold to a third party, they are, you might expect, priced to reflect the increased risks they bear as compared to the senior securities.

35

BOND RATINGS

The purpose of bond ratings is to help investors assess the likelihood that bond debt will be repaid. Several major ratings agencies, including Moody's and Standard & Poor's, have developed methodologies for evaluating the quality of corporate bonds. While the precise methodology used by these agencies may differ somewhat, each agency attempts to measure the likelihood of repayment based on an evaluation of the financial health and performance of the bond issuer.

Moody's. Moody's Investor's Services, Inc., has nine categories of bond ratings, ranging from Aaa, the highest rating attainable, to C, representing the lowest rate by class of bonds. The following is a quoted summary of each of the nine Moody's bond ratings.

Aaa
"Bonds that are rated Aaa are judged to be of the best quality. They carry the smallest degree of investment risk and are generally referred to as *gilt edge*. Interest payments are protected by a large or by an exceptionally stable margin and principal is secure. While the various protective elements are likely to change, such changes as can be visualized are most unlikely to impair the fundamentally strong position of such issues."

Aa
"Bonds that are rated Aa are judged to be of high quality by all standards. Together with the Aaa group they comprise what are generally known as high-grade bonds. They are rated lower than the best bonds because margins of protection may not be as large as in Aaa secu-

rities or fluctuation of protective elements may be of greater amplitude or there may be other elements present which make the long-term risks appear somewhat larger than in Aaa securities."

A

"Bonds that are rated A possess many favorable investment attributes and are to be considered as upper medium grade obligations. Factors giving security to principal and interest are considered adequate but elements may be present which suggest a susceptibility to impairment sometime in the future."

Baa

"Bonds that are rated Baa are considered as medium grade obligations, i.e., they are neither highly protected nor poorly secured. Interest payments and principal security appear adequate for the present but certain protective elements may be lacking or may be characteristically unreliable over any great length of time. Such bonds lack outstanding investment characteristics and in fact have speculative characteristics as well."

Ba

"Bonds that are rated Ba are judged to have speculative elements; their future cannot be considered as well-assured. Often the protection of interest and principal payments may be very moderate and thereby not well safeguarded during both good and bad times over the future. Uncertainty of position characterizes bonds in this."

B

"Bonds which are rated B generally lack characteristics of the desirable investment. Assurance of interest and principal payments or of maintenance of other terms of the contract over any long period of time may be small."

Caa

"Bonds which are rated Caa are of poor standing. Such issues may be in default or there may be present elements of danger with respect to principal or interest."

Ca

"Bonds which are rated Ca represent obligations which are speculative in a high degree. Such issues are often in default or have other marked shortcomings."

C

"Bonds which are rated C are the lowest rated class of bonds, and issues so rated can be regarded as having extremely poor prospects of ever attaining any real investment standing."

In 1989 Moody's completed a study of bond default rates in order to judge whether its bond ratings helped to predict bond default. The study included data from 1941 to the 1980s and confirmed that, as a general proposition, a lower bond rating correlated with higher default rates. However, no system of ratings is perfect. The value of a bond may be affected by events that were unforeseen, and therefore not taken into account by the ratings agencies. For example, when the investment banking firm of Kohlberg, Kravis & Roberts acquired the RJR Nabisco Company for over $20 billion in early 1989 by using, among other vehicles, high-yield bonds known as *junk bonds,* holders of existing RJR bonds found, to their dismay, that the value of their holdings fell dramatically. The market appeared to judge RJR less capable of paying off the older bonds once the company acquired more than $20 billion in new bond debt.

Moody's Municipal Bond Ratings. For municipal bonds, which are bonds issued by state, city, or other nonfederal governmental entities, Moody's uses the same nine categories of ratings that apply to corporate bonds, plus a few special ratings that are used only for municipal bonds. The exclusively municipal bond ratings category is as follows.

"Bonds for which the security depends upon the completion of some act or the fulfillment of some condition are rated conditionally. These are bonds secured by (a) earnings of projects under construction, (b) earnings of projects unseasoned in operating experience (c) rentals which begin when facilities are completed, or (d) payments to which some other limiting condition attaches. Parenthetical rating denotes probable credit stature upon completion of construction or elimination of basis of condition."

Standard & Poor's. S&P also publishes bond ratings, in somewhat different form than does Moody's.

AAA
"Debt rated AAA has the highest rating assigned by Standard & Poor's. Capacity to pay interest and repay principal is extremely strong."

AA
"Debt rated AA has a very strong capacity to pay interest and repay principal and differs from the highest rated issues only in small degree."

A
"Debt rated A has a strong capacity to pay interest and repay principal although it is somewhat more susceptible to the adverse effects of changes in circumstances and economic conditions than debt in higher rated categories."

BBB
"Debt rated BBB is regarded as having an adequate capacity to pay interest and repay principal. Whereas it normally exhibits adequate protection parameters, adverse economic conditions or changing circumstances

are more likely to lead to a weakened capacity to pay interest and repay principal for debt in this category than in higher rated categories."

BB
B
CCC
CC

"Debt rated BB, B, CCC, or CC is regarded, on balance, as predominantly speculative with respect to capacity to pay interest and repay principal in accordance with the terms of the obligation. BB indicates the lowest degree of speculation and CC the highest degree of speculation. While such debt will likely have some quality and protective characteristics, these are outweighed by large uncertainties or major risk exposures to adverse conditions."

C

"This rating is reserved for income bonds on which no interest is being paid."

D

"Debt rated D is in default, and payment of interest and/or repayment of principal is in arrears."

(+)
or
(−)

"The ratings from AA or CCC may be modified by the addition of a plus or minus sign to show relative standing within the major rating categories.

"Continuance of the rating is contingent upon S&P's receipt of an executed copy of the escrow agreement or closing documentation confirming investments and cash flows."

NR

"Indicates no rating has been requested, that there is insufficient information on which to base a rating, or that S&P does not rate a particular type of obligation as a matter of policy.

"Debt obligations of issuers outside the United States and its territories are rated on the same basis as domestic corporate and municipal issues. The ratings measure the creditworthiness of the obligor but do not take into account currency exchange and related uncertainties.

"Bond investment quality standards: Under present commercial bank regulations issued by the Comptroller of the Currency, bonds rated in the top four categories (AAA, AA, A, BBB) commonly are known as *investment grade* bonds and are regarded as eligible for bank investment. In addition, the laws for various states governing legal investments impose certain rating and other standards on obligations eligible for investment by savings banks, trust companies, insurance companies, and fiduciary entities.

"Provisional ratings: The letter p on the rating indicates that the rating is provisional. A provisional rating assumes the successful completion of the project being financed by the debt being rated and indicates that payment of debt service requirements is largely or entirely dependent upon the successful and timely completion of the project. This rating, however, while addressing credit quality subsequent to completion of the project, makes no comment on the likelihood of, or the risk of default upon failure of, such completion. The investor should exercise judgement with respect to such likelihood and risk."

Words of Warning About Ratings. Although bond ratings represent an assessment by the ratings agencies of the quality of the bonds, the ratings are not recommendations that you buy or sell the bonds. Consider ratings only a part of your overall examination of the fitness of the investment. And if you are less sanguine about a company's prospects of repaying the bond than the ratings indicate, err to the side of caution.

36

SCAMS, SWINDLES, AND FOLLIES

Securities scams have been around as long as securities themselves have existed. In addition to scams and swindles involving outright fraud, there are numerous examples of investment disasters that have occurred as a result of innocent folly. Because ultimately your best protection against swindles is your alertness and investment memory, and because the more you know, the more alert you are apt to be, this Key should be referred to more than once in your investment experience. The most prevalent scam in the world of investments is what is known as a *Ponzi scheme*. In a typical Ponzi scheme a company issues securities for what is essentially a ghost enterprise. There is usually little or no real operation as advertised; instead, the issuer sells the securities, takes the money, and spends it on noncompany-related, usually personal, things. In order to keep the house of cards enterprise in place, early investors who want to redeem their securities are usually paid off quickly.

The South Sea Bubble. The South Sea Bubble scandal is a story that has been told many times. Dating from eighteenth-century England, it has lost none of its relevance to investors over the years. The South Sea Company was founded in 1711 to carry on a slave trade and other trade with Spanish America. Based on the belief that slave ownership would soon be legalized by Spain, investors flocked to South Sea Company stock. The company was only moderately successful for its first six years of existence. Fortune smiled on the enterprise in 1718, when King George I became governor of the company, a move that inspired investor confidence in the company's future prospects. More investors flocked to the company, and in 1720 their demand for the stock turned into a full-blown speculative mania.

So confident was the company of its golden future that it proposed (and Parliament accepted) to assume a large part of the national debt. The price of a share soared from 128½ pounds in January of 1720 to 1,000 pounds by August. In the frenzy, many people too poor to absorb stock losses, and who should not have been encouraged to buy stock, were pushed into disastrous investments by promoters and swindlers selling dreams and rosy pictures. Then the bubble burst. In September the stock price began to plummet, and by December shares were trading at around 124. Many investors— small and large, prominent and ordinary—were financially ruined. Ever since, the Bubble scandal has been almost a parable of the dangers in the theory of investing that believes in following the crowd: If so many people are doing it, they can't all be wrong!

Lest you think the South Sea Bubble investors were victims of a naïveté uncharacteristic of the modern investor, here's a story of a more recent vintage.

The ZZZZ Best Story. As a teenager, in 1981, Barry Minkow started ZZZZ Best, a carpet-cleaning service, in his parent's garage. His was a classic American success story. Just four years after starting the company, Minkow had enough to buy a $698,000 home in California, a red Ferrari, and even a poolside doghouse with a vaulted ceiling. Then, like many entrepreneurs before him, Minkow enlisted Wall Street's help to reach the pocket-books of investors across the country: He went public. From the time ZZZZ Best went public in January of 1986 until early 1987, its stock more than quadrupled from $4 a share to $18 per share, creating enormous paper wealth for Minkow and others. There was only one catch to the story. The lucrative carpet-cleaning contracts on which the company based its reported profits were more illusion than reality. In fact, Minkow later admitted that 90 percent of the $43 million in profits reported to investors was nonexistent.

How did Minkow swindle so many? He faked documents and staged phone calls, creating a world that was based on lies. As an explanation of why he defrauded so many investors, Minkow maintains that he was forced to swindle by organized crime figures who literally beat him into cooperating. Where did the money go? Certainly, some of it went to maintain Minkow's lavish lifestyle.

A scam such as ZZZZ Best is a reminder that even some sophisticated Wall Street investment bankers can be defrauded by smoke and mirrors. But even Minkow's scam is small potatoes compared with the story of Thomas Quinn.

The Thomas Quinn Story. Thomas Quinn knew how to turn a buck. He started his biggest swindle in the 1980s with shell companies—corporations with few or no assets—registered in Liechtenstein or Switzerland. His high-pressure salespeople sold the securities of these foreign-registered shell companies by telephone out of boiler rooms set up in the United States. Quinn gave the boiler rooms impressive names such as Falcon Trust, Prudentrust, and Gibraltar Financial Consultants. Their particular prey was investors in the Middle East, Hong Kong, and Australia. Many of the investors are reported to have been retired people with small savings and little experience in the stock market.

Quinn and his associates defrauded investors around the world of more than $500 million before he was arrested on July 27, 1988, at his $6 million pink villa overlooking Cannes in the south of France. This was not his first swindle. Early in 1966 Quinn had been barred by the SEC for life from doing business with any broker or dealer as a result of other frauds. One of his scams involved promoting a company called Kent Industries, which reportedly owned Florida real estate worth millions but that was later discovered to have almost no assets.

A pattern emerges in a review of the stories of many of the major securities swindles. Often the con men are repeat offenders. As an SEC commissioner recently observed, there is a high rate of recidivism by the perpetrators of certain securities frauds.

Investor Protection. While no one can devise a system that is invincible to swindlers, there are practices that, if followed diligently, can help to lower the probability that you will end up a victim of securities fraud. Remember that the key to the success of most swindles is that the schemers have all the information concerning the value of the stock they are selling, and investors, many of whom are geographically remote from the production facilities of the issuing company, have little or no opportunity to verify firsthand the quality—or even the existence—of the issuing company. Investors, therefore, often have no way of actually kicking the tires before buying the car.

The problem is, how do you know if you are buying a stock that is grossly overvalued or worthless? Here are some tips.

1. *For Public Companies Registered with the SEC.* The SEC requires the issuers of stock in public companies to register and make available for public inspection information on the principals of the company, their backgrounds, and the nature of the company's business. Moreover, as we explain in more detail in Key 41, the law requires such companies to update periodically the information initially provided the SEC. This information is available through the company, SEC offices, or *www.sec.gov/edgarhp.htm,* which contains company reports and updates in the Edgar database. For further information, the SEC's Investor Education and Assistance Office in Washington, D.C., can be reached at (202) 942-7040, and its

public information office at e-mail address:
publicinfo@sec.gov
Company information can also be obtained through:
www.freeedgar.com

2. *Other Published Reports.* In addition to the information available through the SEC, you may be able to cull information concerning companies that have been in existence for some time through private information services, including:
   - Nexis, a computerized clipping service that is marketed principally to lawyers
   - Dun & Bradstreet credit rating and financial services
   - Standard & Poor's Registers
   - Moody's Corporate News
   - ICC British Company Directory

These services are too expensive for most individual small investors, but your broker or lawyer may have access to them.

3. *Other Broker Information Services.* If you are using a broker, he or she should have access to files or computerized databases with information on publicly owned companies. In evaluating a broker's recommendations, you should ask which sources were used in compiling their information. Glib answers or impatience should not put you off; these reactions may be merely masking ignorance about the company. A significant amount of company information can be found on a number of on-line investment company sites (see Key 40, On-line Investment Resources). Certain securities are sold to investors on a yield basis. That is, the broker or seller of the security represents to the investor that the security will yield—or is reasonably certain to yield—a certain amount of interest or profit. If a security is sold on this basis, the seller is required to provide the yield along with sufficient information for the investor to understand

the basis and the significance of the figures. It is important that you understand all of the material pricing assumptions before you make a purchase. Don't hesitate to ask questions. It is the broker's job to answer them fully.

4. *Prospectus Examination.* In dealing with a new issue, the prospectus should also provide you with a description of the structure of the security, background information on the issuing company and its principals, as well as the assumptions on which pricing was based. Many people are intimidated by the thickness of a prospectus or the legal language in which many prospectuses are wrapped. If you are considering a major investment, you should consult your attorney. He or she should be able to review the prospectus with you and highlight areas of concern. In any case, bear in mind that the writers of these prospectuses typically are no brighter than you, and if something doesn't make sense to you, you shouldn't assume that the reason is because it is over your head. The real reason may be that the analysis is flawed or the presentation is unclear, in which case you should be persistent in finding out exactly what is meant. And if you don't understand the substance of the prospectus, be wary of making an investment. The pricing and performance predictions may be based on assumptions you don't understand well enough even to question.

5. *Increasing Your Savvy in General.* Unless you are sophisticated (lucky?) enough to time markets or comfortable (daring?) enough to make random selections, you should try to ascertain the true value of the security being offered to you. First of all, the price should bear a reasonable relationship to the value of the products or services sold by the company. Nebulous descriptions of the company's purpose, prospects, or contacts are never accept-

able. Remember that you are not buying just the name of a CEO (even if that name belongs to a king), you are buying the CEO's ability to manage the company effectively. It is also important to develop a working knowledge of the everyday language and concepts of investing, even if you rely on a broker to do your investing for you.

37

THE SECURITIES AND EXCHANGE COMMISSION

The Securities and Exchange Commission (SEC) is the federal agency responsible for monitoring compliance by those who participate in the securities markets to see that the federal securities laws are obeyed. The SEC headquarters are located at 450 Fifth Street, N.W., Washington, D.C. 20549. (The SEC's branch offices are listed at the end of this Key.)

The SEC has five commissioners, and no more than three of the commissioners may come from the same political party. The commissioners are appointed by the president, with the advice and consent of the Senate, and serve for staggered five-year terms. The commission has five divisions:

1. The Division of Corporate Regulations, which is responsible for monitoring compliance under the Public Utility Act and other functions.
2. The Division of Corporation Finance, which is responsible for processing registration statements filed under the 33 Act, the 34 Act, and the 40 Act (see Keys 42–44).
3. The Division of Investment Management, which is responsible for monitoring compliance with the 40 Act and the Investment Advisers Act.
4. The Division of Market Regulation, which is responsible for monitoring and regulating exchanges, market activities, and broker dealers. (This division was responsible for analyzing the

behavior of the exchanges in the Crash of 1987; see its outstanding report, "The October 1987 Market Break.")

5. The Division of Enforcement, which is responsible for enforcement against those found to have violated the federal securities laws. Often, companies that are not sure whether a proposed action will violate the federal securities laws ask the staff of the Division of Enforcement to take what is called a *no-action position* with respect to the proposed activities.

In addition to the divisions above, the Office of the Chief Accountant in the Office of the General Counsel are powerful offices within the commission and often get involved in interpreting whether compliance criteria have been met.

SEC REGIONAL AND DISTRICT OFFICES

The e-mail boxes noted for each of the SEC regional offices listed below may be used to send inquiries, communications, or requests for information about the work of that specific regional office, to report suspected violations of federal securities laws, or if you suspect you have been the victim of a securities-related fraud committed in the states covered by that specific regional office.

1. **Northeast Regional Office—New York and New Jersey**
   Securities and Exchange Commission
   Carmen J. Lawrence
   7 World Trade Center, Suite 1300
   New York, NY 10048
   (212) 748-8000
   e-mail: *newyork@sec.gov*
2. **Boston District Office—Connecticut, Maine, Massachusetts, New Hampshire, Vermont, and Rhode Island**
   Juan M. Marcelino, District Administrator

73 Tremont Street, Suite 600
Boston, MA 02108-3912
(617) 424-5900
e-mail: *boston@sec.gov*

3. **Philadelphia District Office—Delaware, District of Columbia, Maryland, Pennsylvania, Virginia, and West Virginia**
Ronald C. Long, District Administrator
The Curtis Center, Suite 1120E
601 Walnut Street
Philadelphia, PA 19106-3322
(215) 597-3100
e-mail: *philadelphia@sec.gov*

4. **Southeast Regional Office—Florida, Puerto Rico, and the U.S. Virgin Islands**
Randall J. Fons
1401 Brickell Avenue, Suite 200
Miami, FL 33131
(305) 536-4700
e-mail: *miami@sec.gov*

5. **Atlanta District Office—Alabama, Georgia, Louisiana, Mississippi, North Carolina, and Tennessee**
Richard P. Wessel, District Administrator
3475 Lenox Road, N.E., Suite 1000
Atlanta, GA 30326-1232
(404) 842-7600
e-mail: *atlanta@sec.gov*

6. **Midwest Regional Office—Illinois, Indiana, Iowa, Kentucky, Michigan, Minnesota, Missouri, Ohio, and Wisconsin**
Mary Keefe, Regional Director
Citicorp Center, Suite 1400
500 W. Madison Street
Chicago, IL 60661-2511
(312) 353-7390
e-mail: *chicago@sec.gov*

7. **Central Regional Office—Colorado, Nebraska, New Mexico, North Dakota, South Dakota, and Wyoming**
Daniel F. Shea, Regional Director
1801 California Street, Suite 4800
Denver, CO 80202-2648
(303) 844-1000
e-mail: *denver@sec.gov*
8. **Fort Worth District Office—Arkansas, Kansas, Oklahoma, and Texas**
Harold F. Degenhardt, District Administrator
801 Cherry Street, 19th Floor
Fort Worth, TX 76102
(817) 978-3821
e-mail: *dfw@sec.gov*
9. **Salt Lake District Office—Utah**
Kenneth D. Israel, Jr., District Administrator
500 Key Bank Tower, Suite 500
50 South Main Street
Salt Lake City, UT 84144-0402
(801) 524-5796
e-mail: *saltlake@sec.gov*
10. **Pacific Regional Office—Southern California, Arizona, Nevada, Hawaii, and Guam**
Valerie Caproni, Regional Director
5670 Wilshire Boulevard, 11th Floor
Los Angeles, CA 90036-3648
(323) 965-3998
e-mail: *losangeles@sec.gov*
11. **San Francisco District Office—Northern California, Washington, Oregon, Alaska, Idaho, and Montana**
(vacant), District Administrator
44 Montgomery Street, Suite 1100
San Francisco, CA 94104
(415) 705-2500
e-mail: *sanfrancisco@sec.gov*

38

SECURITIES MARKETS

Securities markets deal primarily with stocks and bonds. The purpose of a security market is primarily for businesses to acquire investment capital. Examples of securities markets include the New York Stock Exchange (NYSE), the Nasdaq Stock Market (Nasdaq), and the American Stock Exchange (Amex).

Not all stock markets are the same. They vary by company listing requirements, to begin trading, and maintenance standards, to continue trading, as well as by their rules and regulations governing trading, reporting, and settlement. In addition, all of these exchanges operate in accordance with federal laws, administered by the Securities and Exchange Commission (SEC). Stock markets also vary according to market structure.

The Nasdaq. The Nasdaq Stock Market is electronic screen-based versus the New York Stock Exchange and the American Stock Exchange, which are floor-based. An electronic screen-based market, such as Nasdaq, enables participants to trade stocks with each other through a telecommunications network. They access the market on their desktop terminals anywhere they happen to be located. In the case of floor-based markets, orders are received from brokers—frequently electronically—and are executed by floor traders physically on the exchange floor.

In 1998 the Nasdaq and the American stock exchanges were merged to become the Nasdaq-Amex Market Group under the parent company the National Association of Security Dealers, Inc. (NASD). These exchanges, however, still operate independently.

NYSE. The NYSE is the most prestigious of the three

major markets, and most of the country's larger and older major public companies are traded on this exchange. In general, smaller companies trade on the Amex, whereas Nasdaq has a mix of large and small companies, the majority of them newer companies than those on the NYSE.

A unit of trading in NYSE stocks is 100 shares, called a *round lot,* except for certain stocks designated by the NYSE for trading in a smaller number of shares. Because investors often cannot afford to place orders with brokers for 100 share units, a niche has developed for dealers that specialize in trading in lots of less than 100 shares, called *odd lots.*

Brokers who are members of the NYSE can sell odd lots to a NYSE specialist who in turn will assemble the odd lots into a round lot for trading. Investors who buy odd lots typically pay extra compensation to their brokers. However, some of the larger brokerage houses do not charge odd lot fees on some stocks because they keep sufficient numbers of these stocks in inventory, in effect making a market for these stocks.

Listings. Nasdaq is the largest of the three exchanges, listing more than 5,100 companies in 1998, with NYSE listing 3,114 companies. In terms of market capitalization NYSE led the pack in 1998 at $10 trillion, with Nasdaq next at $2.5 trillion. In numbers of shares traded, 202 billion shares, with a value of $5.8 trillion, were traded on the Nasdaq exchange, and 170 billion shares, with a value of $7.3 trillion, were traded on the NYSE exchange.

Nasdaq has two exchanges, the larger being the Nasdaq National Market, which caters to larger companies with 4,100 securities listed, and the Nasdaq SmallCap Market, which is suited to newer smaller companies and has listings of some 1,400 securities.

OTCBB. Another securities trading system is known as the Over the Counter Bulletin Board (OTCBB) market. Although it does not have any business relationship with NASD, it is regulated by that exchange. The

OTCBB displays real-time quotes, last sale prices, and volume information for more than 6,500 securities. The OTCBB includes those stocks not listed on Nasdaq, Amex, NYSE, or any other national stock market. OTCBB stocks are sometimes known as *pink sheet* stocks. Pink sheets are still published weekly by the National Quotation Bureau. An electronic version of the pink sheets is updated once a day and disseminated over market data vendor terminals.

Investors should be very careful trading in these stocks, since they are from smaller, newer companies with an attendant higher risk.

Problem with a Broker. What happens if an investor gives an order to a broker and the broker somehow gets it wrong? None of the exchanges will take responsibility for executing instructions that are inaccurate because of broker error. Therefore, disputes concerning wrong information will have to be settled between you and your broker.

If you have a problem with your broker or your account:

1. Promptly talk to the broker's manager, or the company's compliance officer.
2. Confirm your complaint in writing.
3. Keep good records.
4. If the problem cannot be solved to your satisfaction at this level, contact the appropriate regulators listed below. Each of these organizations operates a forum to resolve disputes between brokerage firms and their customers.
5. You may wish to consult an attorney knowledgeable about securities laws.

The following is a list of the major U.S. stock exchanges with addresses and phone numbers.

American Stock Exchange, Inc.
86 Trinity Place
New York, NY 10006
(212) 306-1452

Boston Stock Exchange, Inc.
One Boston Place
Boston, MA 02108
(617) 723-9500

Chicago Board Options Exchange, Inc.
400 LaSalle Street
Chicago, IL 60605
(312) 786-7705

Chicago Stock Exchange, Inc.
400 LaSalle Street
Chicago, IL 60605
(312) 663-2222

Cincinnati Stock Exchange, Inc.
205 Dixie Terminal Building
Cincinnati, OH 45202
(513) 621-1410

Municipal Securities Rulemaking Board
1150 18th Street, N.W., Suite 400
Washington, DC 20036
(202) 223-9347

National Association of Securities Dealers, Inc.
1735 K Street
Washington, DC 20036
(301) 590-6500

New York Stock Exchange, Inc.
11 Wall Street
New York, NY 10005
(212) 656-3000

NASD/NASD Regulation, Inc.
1390 Picard Drive
Rockville, MD 20850
(301) 590-6500

Pacific Stock Exchange
301 Pine Street
San Francisco, CA 94104
(415) 393-4000

Philadelphia Stock Exchange, Inc.
1900 Market Street
Philadelphia, PA 19103
(215) 496-5000

Future Plans. Regarding future plans of these exchanges, the NYSE has announced that it is considering becoming a public company, and Nasdaq has announced plans to move into the international arena starting with Nasdaq-Japan based in Tokyo, slated to open in June 2000. Nasdaq is awaiting agreement from the Canadian government to start Nasdaq-Canada in Toronto, and has been having discussions with various entities in Europe regarding setting up a Nasdaq exchange in Europe, possibly in 2001.

The NYSE and Nasdaq exchanges have both announced that they are extending trading hours in 2000.

The SEC has promoted a change from fractional pricing to decimal pricing (dollars and cents) for all exchanges, and have proposed an implementation date of June 30, 2000. All exchanges are working toward that goal.

39

INTERNET ON-LINE TRADING

Trading on-line through the Internet is an increasingly popular and inexpensive method of trading for the individual investor. It is estimated that 16 percent of all stock trades and 4 percent of all bond trades in the United States are executed through on-line trading.

Investors can buy or sell securities through on-line securities trading companies such as E*Trade, Ameritrade, Datek, DLJ Direct, ScoTTrade, Accutrade, Suretrade, Wall St Access, Web St, and CompuTEL Securities. Costs per trade for these on-line brokerages range (in 1999) from $5 to $20 per trade. There is usually a limit on the number of shares (frequently 5,000 shares) that can be traded for this transaction price.

Many discount and other brokerages such as Charles Schwab, Quick & Reilly, Merrill Lynch, Fidelity, and Knight/Trimark Group now offer on-line trading to their clients. These brokerages offer more investor services, and cost more per trade. Typical range in 1999 is $30 to $50 per trade. Full-service brokerages provide more services and charge considerably more.

A confirmation that your requested trade has been executed will be displayed on your screen and will also normally be surface-mailed or e-mailed to you. Stock certificates in this case are usually held on your behalf by the on-line trading company or designated transfer agent. You can obtain physical possession of your certificates by requesting them from the brokerage or transfer agent, for an additional charge.

If you plan to purchase a stock on-line, in most cases

you must have enough cash in the brokerage account to cover the trade. You can borrow funds using securities held by your broker as collateral to cover the cost of a stock purchase. This is called *buying on margin.*

Some brokerages offer extended hours trading, before and after the traditional markets open and close. These trades are executed through alternative Internet trading systems, and frequently limit the type and number of stocks that can be traded.

Another method of trading offered by many brokerages is an automated touch tone telephone system. Charges for this method are generally higher than for on-line trading.

40

ON-LINE INVESTMENT RESOURCES

Some of the sites noted below offer free research, advice, investment portfolio tracking, and on-line account information, and some require fees for certain of their services. Many require registration even if the products are free. Many of the sites offer most or all of the services in each category, but are listed only under the primary service they offer.

There are many more Internet sites, too numerous to list here, that offer similar products and services. It is likely that on-line financial services and on-line trading will experience explosive growth in the next few years (2000–2005) and it is anticipated that Internet on-line securities trading will become the major method of buying and selling securities in the next decade.

Research and Advice:
Charles Schwab
www.schwab.com—Real-time quotes, research data.
DailyStocks
www.dailystocks.com—Company and market research, investment advice.
FreeEDGAR
www.freeedgar.com—Access to Securities and Exchange filings made by companies.
Gomez Advisors
www.gomezadvisors.com—Research firm ratings, and broker rankings.

InvesTools
   www.investools.com—Research reports, company
   news.
Morningstar
   www.morningstar.net—Extensive stock and fund
   research.
The Motley Fool
   www.fool.com—Message boards allow investors to
   meet and get advice.
OnlineInvestors.com
   www.onlineinvestors.com—Ratings of discount brokers.
SEC EDGAR
   www.sec.gov/edgarhp.htm—Database of corporate
   filings made by public companies.
The Silicon Investor
   www.techstocks.com—Advice on technology stocks.
Thomson Real-Time Quotes
   www.thomsonrtq.com—Free real-time stock quotes,
   company reports.
Wall Street Research Net
   www.wsrn.com—Links to stock research, fundamental data.
Zacks
   www.zacks.com—Real-time quotes, analyses, broker
   reports.

Portfolio Tracking:
America on Line
   www.aol.com—Portfolio tracking, real-time quotes.
TDWaterhouse
   www.tdwaterhouse.com—Portfolio tracking, real-
   time quotes.
Charles Schwab
   www.schwab.com—Portfolio tracking, real-time
   quotes.
The Thomson Investors Network—
   www.marketedge.com—Portfolio tracking, real-time
   quotes.

Quick & Reilly
  www.qronline.com—Portfolio tracking, real-time quotes.

Discount On-line Trading:
Accutrade
  www.accutrade.com—On-line trading, light research.
American Express
  www.americanexpressonline.com
Ameritrade
  www.ameritrade.com—On-line trading, research, portfolio tracking.
Datek On-line
  www.datek.com—On-line trading, light research, portfolio tracking, extended hours trading.
DLJ Direct
  www.dljdirect.com—On-line trading, light research, portfolio tracking, extended hours trading.
E*Trade
  www.etrade.com—On-line trading, research, portfolio tracking, extended hours trading.
ScoTTrade
  www.scottrade.com—On-line trading, research.
Suretrade
  www.suretrade.com—On-line trading, light research.

Full Service Brokers with On-line Services:
Fidelity
  www.fidelity.com—On-line trading, portfolio tracking, research.
Merrill Lynch
  www.merrilllynch.com—Research, portfolio tracking.
Morgan Stanley Dean Witter
  www.online.msdw.com—On-line trading, research, extended hours trading, 24-hour telephone trading, portfolio tracking.

Paine Webber
  www.painewebber.com—On-line trading, research,
  portfolio tracking.
Salomon Smith Barney
  www.salomonsmithbarney.com—On-line trading,
  research, portfolio tracking, extended hours trading.

41

MAJOR FEDERAL SECURITIES LAWS

Too long has high finance been low business...For a horse trade where the buyer has full opportunity to examine his purchase "Let the buyer beware" was a good rule...When to the natural complexities of pyramiding holding companies is added the wizardry and worse some types of Financial priestcraft, even the most alert buyer has little chance.—Christian Science Monitor, as quoted in the 73rd Congress Congressional Record.

Securities are regulated by both the federal government and each of the 50 states. In this book, we focus only on the federal scheme of regulation, and leave the 50-state survey of state securities regulation for another text.

The key to understanding federal securities regulation is always to remember that Uncle Sam *does not regulate the soundness or quality of the securities of private companies offered to the investing public.* Many investors do not realize that the government is not in the business of making sure buyers are only offered safe, conservative investments. Many investors do not realize that sellers are free to offer buyers securities as safe as cash or as volatile as nitroglycerin.

The SEC requires only that sellers tell their buyers whatever is important about the security. It's left to buyers to exercise good business judgment in deciding whether to purchase a security once all the facts have been disclosed.

There are six major federal securities laws.

1. the Securities Act of 1933 (the 33 Act)
2. the Securities Exchange Act of 1934 (the 34 Act)
3. the Investment Company Act of 1940 (the 40 Act)

4. the Investment Advisers Act
5. the Trust Indenture Act of 1939
6. the Public Utility Company Holding Act of 1935

Much of what should be understood about securities and much of the natural tension between buyers and sellers of securities and between brokers and customers, depends for context on the policies that have shaped the regulation of securities.

In the individual Keys that follow, we review the laws and policies that have been fashioned to protect buyers of securities and the perils these laws and policies are intended to thwart.

42

THE SECURITIES ACT OF 1933

[T]oday the owner of shares in a corporation possesses a mere symbol of ownership, while the power, the responsibility, and the substance that have characterized ownership in the past have been transferred to a separate group, which holds control. It is for the protection of these 18 million owners of symbols that this bill has been drawn—*Congressional Record 1933*

The securities market can be divided into the primary market, where initial public offerings and placements occur, and the secondary or trading market, where securities initially registered or placed are traded and retraded to individuals and institutions. The 33 Act is the major federal law regulating the primary securities market, and the 34 Act, which is described in Key 43, is the major federal law regulating the secondary securities market.

In the late 1920s the American public invested millions of dollars in securities that lost most of their value from 1929 to 1932. In what has come to be viewed as a sure sign of stock mania, everyone from high-priced executives to taxi drivers "played the market." The huge losses suffered from the collapse of the stock market, the bank runs, and the bread lines of the Depression prompted Congress to act to protect the investing public against financial abuses. At the time of the 1929 Crash most states already had in place securities laws to protect their citizens, but the losses on investments continued to mount. Among the abuses cited by congressional investigators was the practice of some securities firms that sold securities from a location in state A to residents of a regulated state B to avoid compliance with B's laws.

Responding to the need to provide a federal regulation net broad enough to catch practices outside the reach of any individual state, the Congress was faced with the decision of how to regulate. There were two major choices.

1. Regulation of the *kinds* of securities that can be offered to the public, thus creating a list of "approved" investments and a list of "forbidden" investments: this scheme was followed by many state *blue sky securities laws.*

2. Regulation of the market by permitting issuers to sell any type of security they wish as long as the public is given full and accurate disclosure of all information needed to make an intelligent purchase decision.

The second scheme is the one adopted by the Congress for the 33 Act and the other federal securities laws in general. The driving philosophy was disclosure without sanction: Put all the facts about the investment before the buyer and leave it to the buyers to decide whether it's in their best interests to make a risky investment or a conservative one. Nevertheless, it is important that prospective buyers of a security never view the registration of a security with the SEC, or a declaration that a security is exempt from registration, as an official government stamp of approval of the security's soundness and quality.

The perception in the Congress was that many investors could have been spared financial devastation had market practices been more closely monitored. "We believe it would have saved thousands of people from the losses incident to a wild orgy of speculation...If there had been such a law, thousands of widows and orphans would not today be saddened and crushed."

Predating by one year the creation of the Securities Exchange Commission, the 33 Act was enacted by Congress in response to such perceived financial scandals and abuses.

Registration Requirements. Before an issuer may use the mails or telephone or any other means of communicating across state lines to sell a security to the public, the issuer must register the security with the SEC and provide prospective purchasers with a prospectus that adequately discloses material information about the securities, unless the security falls within certain narrowly defined exemptions to registration. The issuer must file a registration statement, which becomes effective 20 days following filing unless the SEC deems the statement defective or deficient in some way.

Exemptions. Because registration requirements can be costly, would-be issuers try to fit within certain exemptions listed in the statute. Exemptions may apply to the security or to the issuer of the security. The exemptions for securities include

1. Government-guaranteed securities—securities issued or guaranteed by federal or state governments or their subdivisions or instrumentalities, or banks.
2. Federal Reserve Bank securities—securities issued by or representing an interest in or direct obligation of a Federal Reserve Bank.
3. Limited offering securities—issuances limited to a small number of investors who are financially sophisticated.

Private Placements. Section 4(2) of the 33 Act exempts from registration requirements issuances not made to the public. These are called *private placements.* Thus, by placing securities privately, an issuer may be able to avoid costly registration fees.

Forty years of court cases, regulations, SEC rules, and rules-within-rules have grown up like intertwined vines to form a haphazard structure for interpreting the limitations of the valuable private placement exemption. The SEC has adopted rule 506 to give market participants clearer guidelines on the requirements of the private placement exemption. A central concept of the private placement exemption is that issuances may be made without the registration procedures to certain investors because the financial sophistication of these investors obviates the need for registration and prospectus disclosure. Who can fend for themselves? The SEC rules include in that description

1. certain institutional investors such as banks, insurance companies, investment companies, registered investment advisers, and certain tax-exempt organizations with over $5 million in assets.
2. directors or executive officers of the issuer.
3. any natural person whose individual net worth exceeds $1 million or whose income exceeded $200,000 in the past two years and is reasonably expected to exceed $200,000 in the current year.
4. any person who buys at least $150,000 of the securities being offered for cash so long as the total price paid is less than 20 percent of the joint net worth of the purchaser and the purchaser's spouse.

Investors of the above types are called *accredited,* and no specific disclosure document is required to make sales to such investors. However, sellers to accredited investors are subject to the antifraud provisions of the federal securities laws.

43

THE SECURITIES EXCHANGE ACT OF 1934

Exchanges such as the New York Stock Exchange, the American Stock Exchange, Nasdaq, the over-the-counter (OTC) markets, and the other exchanges all around the world enable investors to trade all types of securities in large volume. Exchanges provide the important element of *liquidity* to the securities markets. A market is said to be ideally liquid if sellers can always find buyers willing to buy, and buyers can find sellers willing to sell. Through exchanges, large numbers of buyers and sellers can communicate orders, easing the flow of capital nationally and internationally.

Although the NYSE, the Amex, and Nasdaq dominate the securities markets in terms of volume traded today, at the time of the passage of the 34 Act, the Congress identified over 30 regional exchanges throughout the nation. The house rules used to regulate trading in each exchange varied widely. The broad aim of the powerful 34 Act was to regulate such rules to prevent those in control of the exchanges or those with financial power enough to exert control from manipulating markets to their own advantage and to the disadvantage of the public. Briefly described below are some of the key exchange practices that led to the passage of the 34 Act.

Margin Practices. In 1934 a committee of the Congress reported that an alarming number of Americans used credit to buy securities. On the New York Stock Exchange, some 42 percent of the customers of the members of that Exchange had margin accounts, and approximately 22 percent of the customers of the member firms of the other exchanges used margin accounts.

How does the margin account work? The basic mechanics are simple: A purchaser establishes a contract with a seller that only requires the purchaser to pay a part of the purchase price in cash, borrowing to finance the balance. If the market value of the securities subsequently exceeds the total cash downpayment plus the amount of the margin loan, the purchaser can realize an extremely high rate of return on cash invested. The purchaser can then sell the securities at market value, pay off the margin loan, and pocket the profit. If the stock goes down, however, the purchaser can be caught in a painful squeeze, as illustrated by the following situation:

EXAMPLE:

Buyer Bob decided to buy 10,000 shares of Z stock at a market price of $5 per share, for a total purchase price of $50,000. Bob entered a margin contract with his broker requiring Bob to make a downpayment of $5,000 in cash, and allowing him to finance the remaining $45,000 of the purchase price with a margin loan from the brokerage house. Ten weeks after the purchase, Z stock had climbed to $10 per share. Had Bob then sold all of his Z stock for a total of $100,000, he would have pocketed a profit of $55,000 on his initial cash investment of $5,000. But Bob didn't sell because Z's stock still had good prospects.

The brokerage house was happy to carry Bob's loan so long as the market value of Z stock exceeded the margin loan plus interest and any miscellaneous fees charged to Bob.

Fifteen weeks after Bob's initial purchase, Z stock began to fall in value. Bob thought the drop was temporary, but he was wrong. Z stock fell to $4 per share, making the market value of Bob's portfolio $40,000. Because the loan of $45,000 exceeded by $5,000 the Z market value of $40,000, the brokerage house asked Bob to cover his margin by depositing $5,000. (The broker might have required even more of a cash injection if it believed the stock had further to fall.) Bob could not afford to lose any more money, so he instructed the broker to sell the stock. Thus, including margin interest and other fees, Bob lost over $10,000.

As the above example shows, margin contracts can expose buyers to substantial portfolio losses. Bob could have limited his exposure by placing a stop loss order, initially perhaps at $4.50 per share, then moving it up as Z stock increased in value. But Bob was an optimist, and he did not think about ways of protecting himself in case of a down turn in the stock.

Based in part on its belief that the high volume of debt made possible by margin accounts fueled stock speculation and accelerated the decline of the financial markets when the debt carried on margin could not be repaid, Congress passed the Securities Exchange Act of 1934.

To limit the amount of debt a buyer of securities may incur, the 34 Act established an extensive set of broker/dealer margin rules that require buyers to invest a certain amount of cash for each dollar financed. Though the margin account was and is a credit account requiring an evaluation of the safe credit tolerance of a would-be borrower, before 1934 many brokers proved ill equipped or unwilling to perform the sometimes tedious tasks needed to evaluate the credit tolerance of the purchaser/borrower.

The danger of this practice of banking by nonbankers was increased because the brokers, through their brokerage houses, and the houses in turn through their banks, had virtually unlimited acess to the gigantic credit resources of the Federal Reserve System. But unlike loans made by banks directly to customers, these broker-loans were not reserved against by banks nor were they controlled by Federal Reserve regulations. As a result, the concentration of lending power in the hands of brokers with financial incentives to increase commissions through making more and more of these loans led to margin accounts bulging with credit vulnerable to liquidation if stock values decreased. Since hindsight is perfect, we can see that the arrangement invited danger and mishap.

The 34 Act dams the uncontrolled flow of credit from the banking system to the securities markets in two ways.

1. If credit is to be used for the purpose of buying securities, such *purpose credit* must be recognized and treated as loans, fully subject to reserve requirements and the range of other consumer protections.
2. To eliminate the possibility that brokers will obtain credit from unregulated lenders, the Act requires that purpose credit only be obtained through the Federal Reserve System.

Insider Practices. Another aim of the 34 Act was to protect public shareholders by prohibiting directors, officers, and principal shareholders from speculating in the stock of corporations to which they owe the special fiduciary duties of loyalty and care. The Act imposes a number of requirements on any person who is a director, officer, or beneficial owner of at least 10 percent of an equity class of security issued by the corporation. The Act requires any such person to

1. report any change in his or her ownership in the corporation's stock
2. account for any profits realized from the purchase and sale of stock within a six-month period
3. refrain from conducting activities that give the appearance of an increased demand for a stock but that in effect do nothing to transfer beneficial ownership in the stock—so called "wash sales"
4. refrain from engaging in a practice called *selling against-the-box* (see Key 8).

Reporting Practices. As mentioned earlier,

exchanges set many of their practices through house rules. In 1934 the Congress discovered that house rules varied widely in many ways, including in the amount of registration information required. Registration requirements also varied, depending on whether the stock was *listed,* meaning that the issuer applied in its own right to have the stock placed on the exchange, or *unlisted,* meaning that the issuer placed the stock on the exchange through an existing member of the exchange, which also was a holder of the issuer's stock. For example, according to Frank Altschul, then chairman of the New York Stock Exchange committee on stock listings, that exchange in 1934 exhaustively examined the facts contained in an issuer's initial application for a listing. But for subsequent applications made by an issuer that had previously listed securities, the examination was more cursory.

To give public shareholders the same access as insiders to information about the issuer's financial condition, the 34 Act requires an issuer with securities registered on an exchange to provide information on its financial condition, and to periodically update the information. Today, the 34 Act applies both to (1) securities listed on a national exchange and (2) unlisted securities issued by a corporation with a net worth exceeding $3 million issuing a class of securities with more than 500 equity shareholders of record.

Although as originally enacted, the 34 Act dealt only with practices on exchanges and did not address the over-the-counter (OTC) market, the Act now also regulates that market as well as other entities and professional associations that conduct markets such as the OTC market.

Broker/Dealers. In addition to brokers and dealers, exchanges, and associations, the 34 Act regulates market makers. A *market maker* is defined as a specialist who can act as a dealer to position blocks of stock or who holds himself out as being willing to make a market in a security by buying and selling the security on [an as-needed or] a regular basis.

All broker/dealers must register with the SEC except those only involved in intrastate business or who only trade exempted securities. Registered broker/dealers must also belong to a registered association of securities dealers. Currently, the National Association of Securities Dealers (NASD) is the only such registered association.

The SEC. The 34 Act also created the Securities Exchange Commission, the federal agency responsible for monitoring compliance with the federal securities laws. After its creation, the SEC also acquired authority to monitor compliance with the 33 Act, which in its first year of existence had been regulated by the Federal Trade Commission.

44

THE INVESTMENT COMPANY ACT OF 1940 AND OTHER STATUTES

The Investment Company Act of 1940 applies to any entity meeting the definition of an *investment company.* The Act basically was designed to curb abuses in investment companies by requiring a company to notify the SEC of its existence and activities through registration. An investment company is defined, pursuant to Section 3(a) of the 40 Act, to include an issuer, which

1. is or holds itself out as being engaged primarily, or proposes to engage primarily, in the business of investing, reinvesting, or trading in securities.
2. is engaged or proposes to engage in the business of issuing face-amount certificates of the installment type, or has been engaged in such business and has any such certificates outstanding.
3. is engaged or proposes to engage in the business of investing, reinvesting, owning, holding, or trading in securities, and owns or proposes to acquire investment securities having a value exceeding 40 percent of the value of such issuer's total asset (exclusive of government securities and cash items) on an unconsolidated basis.

To be considered an investment company pursuant to the definitions set forth in Sections 3(a) (1) and 3(a) (3) of the 40 Act, the issuer must have assets that are securities, meeting the definition that was discussed in Key 1.

The 40 Act specifically excludes 13 entities from the definition of investment company. The most commonly used exemptions are

1. issuers whose outstanding securities—other than short-term paper—are beneficially owned, as set forth therein, by not more than 100 persons and that is not making and does not presently propose to make a public offering of its securities.
2. underwriters and broker-dealers of securities.
3. banks, insurance companies, savings and loan associations, and similar institutions.
4. any person substantially all of whose business is confined to making small loans, industrial banking, or similar businesses.
5. certain nonprofit entities.
6. persons
   a. acquiring or purchasing notes, drafts, acceptances, open accounts receivables, and other obligations.
   b. making loans to manufacturers, wholesalers, and retailers of, and to prospective purchasers of, specified merchandise, insurance, and services.
   c. purchasing or otherwise acquiring interests in real estate.

The scheme of the definitions of the 40 Act can seem complex, but a good rule of thumb to remember is that generally most broker/dealers have to register with the SEC. And the prudent view is to operate under the assumption that the issuer's interest is a security that would cause the issuer to be defined as an investment company, unless otherwise clearly exempt.

The Investment Advisers Act. This Act was created to regulate so-called investment advisers, defined as "[A]ny person who, for compensation engages in the business of advising others, either directly or through publications or writings, as to the value of securities or as to the advisability of investing in, purchasing, or selling securities, or who, for compensation and as part of a regular business, issues or promulgates analyses or reports concerning securities."

Specifically excluded from the definition are
1. banks that are not investment companies.
2. certain professionals, including lawyers and accountants who give investment advice solely incidental to the practice of their professions.
3. broker/dealers, so long as the advice they give is incidental to the conduct of their brokerage business and they are specially compensated for their advice.
4. persons limiting their advice to U.S. government securities.
5. publishers of any bonafide newspaper, new magazine, business or financial publication of general and regular circulation.

The Trust Indenture Act of 1939. This Act generally applies to issuances of debt securities to the public and requires that in connection with such issuance, an independent trustee be appointed to protect the interests of the debt security holders. The Act generally requires that the debt securities be issued pursuant to an indenture with terms prescribed by the Act.

The Public Utility Holding Company Act of 1935. This Act was enacted to curb abuses by owners of public utility holding companies in the 1920s and 1930s.

QUESTIONS AND ANSWERS

What are gilt-edged securities?

Gilt means covered or lined with gold. Gilt-edged has come to mean not only objects that are covered or lined along the edges with gold, but also, when used to describe securities, a security of the highest quality. For example, a gilt-edged bond is one issued by a company that has paid interest consistently throughout its history. Common stock of a company with a long and excellent record of paying dividends also can be referred to as gilt-edged, although, with respect to stock and other equity securities, the preferred phrase is *blue chip*.

What is the best way to go about selecting a broker?

For many investors, the telephone is the only contact they have with their brokers. Many investors make investments with a broker after meeting their brokers (or financial advisers) through cold calls, unsolicited telephone calls from the broker to the investor at the investor's workplace or home. Or, prompted by a television commercial or newspaper advertisement, the investor may initiate the relationship over the telephone. After these phone calls, the investor may know little more about the person at the other end of the line than his or her name and whether he or she "sounds pleasant enough."

A good way to select a broker is to cull names from your friends or family who have had good and preferably long investment experiences with their brokers. If this informal survey produces no names, you should obtain a copy from your library of a reference volume listing brokerage houses in your area, their specialties and history. One such volume is Standard & Poor's *Security Dealers of North America.* If you plan on using a full-service broker (and not a discount broker), you will need to go further and visit the brokerage house to get a feel for how the firm operates, and, most important, to conduct an interview of the prospective broker.

The interview of a prospective broker should include, at a minimum, questions about (1) the broker's experience in investing in various products that may interest you, (2) the kind and quality of research the broker or the brokerage house typically conducts before recommending a security for purchase or sale, and (3) any securities-related disciplinary proceedings, arbitrations, or lawsuits in which the broker may have been involved.

You should contact the SEC branch office nearest you (see Key 37) and the state securities regulator to find out whether the broker has been the subject of proceedings or lawsuits. This can now be done on-line through NASD, or by toll-free calls (see Key 38). You should also ascertain the theory of investing the broker follows (see Keys 15 to 18) and the broker's commission schedule. Brokerage houses typically have contracts you must review and sign before opening an account with a broker. On this form, you should indicate what discretion, if any, you wish to give your broker to trade your securities without first consulting with you.

If you do not wish to give your broker *any* discretion to trade on his or her own initiative, you should make this clear, following up your interview with a letter to this effect, if necessary.

What is the difference between a discount broker and a full-service broker?

First, a discount broker charges lower commission rates than a full-service broker, although there are wide variations in both groups. As stated, investors should check rates before opening a brokerage account.

Discount brokers are used principally by investors who want to make their own investment decisions to buy and/or to sell a security or mutual fund. Generally, these brokers execute these orders exactly as they are placed by the customer, without offering advice. Full-service brokers offer a wide range of services to investors, most importantly advice on which stocks, bonds, mutual funds, and other investments appear to be good buys. Thus, this type of broker is of interest to people who want financial advice on their investments (see Key 39 for Internet trading).

What is a prospectus?

A prospectus is a document describing a public security, the company issuing the security, its officers, and the source of funds to pay the obligations created by the security. In essence, the prospectus is the document that should give investors all the important information concerning the way the security is structured as well as any special risks that owning the security will bring. The standard used to decide what information about a security is important (and, therefore, must be included in the prospectus) and what information may be omitted is *materiality.*

While courts and those in the securities industry may differ on what is material in an individual case, as a general matter it is understood that certain kinds of information are material. For example, pricing assumptions, where a security is sold on a yield basis, is material information. The financial condition of the issuer and major lawsuits against the issuer also constitute material information.

For public securities, the prospectus must be registered and must have become effective prior to the sale of securities to investors. The prospectus, which is filed with the SEC, is sometimes called an offering circular, and preliminary prefiling versions of the prospectus are sometimes called *red herrings.* It is important to review the information contained in the prospectus before making an investment decision. Investors sometimes are daunted by the thickness of the prospectus and the legalese it may contain. Nonetheless, the information should be reviewed by the investor and, in cases involving major investments, by his or her attorney or financial adviser as well.

What is a Ginnie Mae?

A Ginnie Mae is a security carrying the guarantee of the Government National Mortgage Association, known by the acronym GNMA, or Ginnie Mae, an arm of the United States Department of Housing and Urban Development.

GNMA guarantees issues of various forms of mortgage-backed securities. This guarantee is backed by the full faith and credit of the United States. As a result, Ginnie Maes are considered risk-free securities. One form of Ginnie Mae security is the pass-through, which is a security representing an ownership interest in a pool. The servicer of the pool passes through the income received from the mortgages to the investor after subtracting a fixed fee payable to Ginnie Mae for its guarantee.

Ginnie Maes are sold in minimum denominations of $25,000 and are available through most major brokerage houses. Mutual funds that invest in Ginnie Maes sometimes have smaller minimum investment requirements.

How do I find out if my bond is callable?

Bonds are issued pursuant to an indenture, which is the basic legal document between investors and the issuer. Among other things, the indenture describes the security supporting the bonds, the convenants, representations, and other promises of the issuer, and appoints a trustee to act as the representative for bondholders to monitor the issuer's compliance with its obligations under the indenture. The terms of the indenture may provide that the bonds are callable (or *redeemable*) by the issuer for certain prices at certain times.

Treasury bills and most Treasury bonds are not callable. For municipal bonds, the terms of the indenture may be summarized in an official statement that lists call dates and call prices.

As a general matter, bondholders are free to write or otherwise contact the trustee or the issuer to ascertain whether their bonds are callable.

What is the difference between a Treasury bill and a Treasury bond?

Treasury bills and Treasury bonds are both debt securities of the United States government. The term *Treasury bill* refers to Treasury securities having maturities from three months to one year. Treasury bonds, on the other hand, can have maturities ranging up to 30 years.

Both Treasury bills and Treasury bonds are sold through an auction process at Federal Reserve Banks. See Key 32 for more information on Treasury bills and Treasury bonds as well as Treasury notes, which are intermediate-term government securities with maturities of 1 to 10 years.

What are ADRs?

ADRs are negotiable certificates representing a certain number of shares of a foreign security. These foreign securities actually are deposited with an institution in the United States, usually a bank or bank affiliate. The ADRs represent some fraction or multiple of the total shares of a foreign company and constitute a depositary receipt enabling the holder to transfer title to the corresponding amount of foreign securities simply by transferring the ADR.

While ADRs are the predominant vehicles used to trade foreign securities in the United States markets, you should bear in mind that certain foreign securities are traded in the United States using a mechanism other than the ADR. For example, Dutch companies sometimes create special classes of common stock structured specifically for the United States market.

How are securities regulated?

Securities are regulated on both the federal and state level. On the federal level, there are six principal statutes. The principal aim of the federal scheme is the disclosure of material information to investors, without dictating to investors which investments are appropriate. After receiving information on securities, the investors are left to use their business judgment to decide whether to invest in conservative or risky securities.

On the state level, each state can decide what kinds of securities regulations to impose. In contrast, unlike the federal scheme, some states list which investments are permissible and which are not permissible for sale.

The Securities and Exchange Commission (SEC) is the federal agency responsible for monitoring compliance with federal securities laws. (See Key 37 for more information on the SEC and its branch offices.) On the state level, each state designates which agency of the state government handles securities regulation.

What are unit investment trusts?

Unit investment trusts (UITs) are large portfolios of securities divided into shares issued to investors. UITs have fixed portfolios in that once the UIT is established, the securities in the portfolio never change until they mature or are called by the issuer. UITs, in contrast to mutual funds, are not managed, and therefore investors in UITs may save management fees.

Like mutual funds, UITs offer investors a chance to diversify their holdings. Because the quality of the UIT depends on the quality of the securities in the portfolio, investors should be careful that they understand the composition of the UIT portfolio. If, for example, the UIT portfolio is made up of zero coupon bonds, the investor would not receive any interest until these bonds mature, yet the IRS would tax the accruing interest component prior to maturity.

The investor should also be wary of how UITs advertise themselves. Mutual funds are subject to new rules prescribing the way in which they may state yields and the content of their advertisements. UITs are not subject to the same regulations.

GLOSSARY

Account executive brokerage firm employee who advises and handles orders for clients. An account executive must be registered with the National Association of Securities Dealers (NASD). Also called *financial adviser, registered representative.*

Accredited investor investor with substantial means who does not count as one of the maximum of 35 people allowed to put money into a private limited partnership. Such an investor must have a net worth of at least $1 million or an annual income of at least $200,000, or must put at least $150,000 into the deal, and the investment must not account for more than 20 percent of the investor's worth.

Accrued interest interest that has accumulated between the most recent interest payment and the sale of a bond or other fixed-income security. At the time of sale, the buyer pays the seller the bond's price plus accrued interest.

Accumulated dividend dividend due, usually to holders of cumulative preferred stock, but not paid.

Acknowledgment verification that a signature on a financial document is legitimate and has been certified by an authorized person.

Acquisition one company taking over another company. *See also* Merger and Takeover.

Adjustable rate mortgage (ARM) mortgage loan on which interest rates are adjusted at regular intervals according to predetermined criteria. An ARM's interest rate is tied to an objective, published interest rate index.

After-tax rate of return rate of return after applicable federal, state, and local income taxes are subtracted from an investment's gain.

All or none (AON) order marked so that only the total number of shares in the order is to be traded, that no partial transactions are to be executed.

American depositary receipt (ADR) receipt for the shares of a foreign corporation held by a U.S. bank. Americans can buy shares in the United States in the form of an ADR.

American depositary shares (ADS) trading unit for the issuer in the United States that may represent more or less than one underlying share of the issuer. They are issued in New York in registered form, eligible for trading and clearing in U.S. markets, and may be made eligible for clearing outside the United States in Euroclear and CEDEL.

American Stock Exchange (Amex) stock exchange with the second biggest volume of trading in the United States. Located in New York, the Amex was known until 1921 as the *Curb Exchange.*

Amortization liquidation of a debt through installment payments.

Analyst employee of a financial institution who studies a number of companies and makes buy or sell recommendations on the securities of particular companies and industry groups.

Any or all order marked so that the shares specified need not be traded together, and partial transactions may be made.

Arbitrage transaction profiting from discrepancies in price when the same item is traded on two or more markets. Another arbitrage strategy is to buy shares in a company that is about to be taken over when the market price is less than the anticipated takeover price.

Asset allocation funds funds that have the ability to shift assets among asset classes, for example, equities, bonds, and short-term instruments. Asset allocation funds take the concept of a private asset manager—a skilled professional who builds and manages a comprehensive portfolio for a client—and applies it to a mutual fund.

Asset-backed securities bonds or notes backed by loan paper or accounts receivable originated by banks, credit card companies, or other providers of credit and often enhanced by a bank letter of credit or by insurance coverage provided by an institution other than the issuer.

Asset management account account at a financial institution that combines banking services such as check-writing with brokerage features such as buying securities.

Auction sealed-bid public sale of Treasury securities, a method of determining the rate or yield.

Average life average amount of time that will elapse from the date of a mortgage-backed security purchase until the principal is repaid based on an assumed prepayment forecast. Alternatively, average life is the average amount of time a dollar of principal is invested in a mortgage-backed security pool.

Back-end load redemption charge an investor pays when drawing money from an investment. Most common in mutual funds.

Back office bank or brokerage house administrative departments not directly involved in selling or trading.

Balanced fund mutual fund that buys common stock, preferred stock, and bonds in an effort to obtain the highest return consistent with relative safety.

Balloon final payment on a debt that is much larger than the preceding payments.

***Barron's* confidence index** weekly index of corporate bond yields published by *Barron's,* comparing *Barron's* average yield on 10 top-grade bonds to the Dow Jones average yield on 40 bonds.

Basis point smallest measure used in quoting yields on bonds and notes. One basis point is 0.01 percent of yield.

Bear investor who thinks a market is likely to fall, thus is likely to be a seller of securities.

Bearer bond bond that is not issued in the name of an investor but carries coupons that may be presented for redemption by the bearer to the issuer or paying agent.

Beneficial owner one who benefits from owning a security, even if the security's title of ownership is in the name of a broker or bank (*street name*).

Beta coefficient measure of a stock's relative volatility to the rest of the stock market; thus, the Standard & Poor's 500 Stock Index has a beta coefficient of 1.

Bid highest price a prospective buyer is prepared to pay at a particular time for a given security.

Block large quantity of stock or large dollar amount of bonds held or traded.

Blue chip nationally known large company that has a long record of profit growth and dividend payment and a reputation for good management, products, and services.

Blue-sky laws laws passed by various states to protect investors against securities fraud, requiring sellers of new stock issues or mutual funds to register their offerings and provide financial details on each issue.

Boiler room business in which high-pressure salespeople use banks of telephones to call lists of potential investors in order to sell speculative, even fraudulent, securities.

Bond any interest-bearing security that obligates the issuer to pay the bondholder a specified sum of money, usually at specific intervals, and to repay the face value of the bond at maturity.

Bond rating method of evaluating the possibility of default by a bond issuer. Standard & Poor's and Moody's are the main rating agencies. Their ratings range from AAA to D.

Book value value at which an asset is carried on a balance sheet or cost when purchased; also, total net asset value of a company.

Broker in the securities field one who acts as an intermediary between a buyer and seller, usually charging a commission.

Bull investor who thinks prices are likely to rise, thus is a buyer of stocks or other securities.

Business day in finance, days when financial markets are open.

Buyout individual group or company's purchase of at least a controlling percentage of a company's stock to take over its assets and operations. A buyout can occur through negotiations or through tender offers.

Callable redeemable by the issuer before the scheduled maturity. The issuer must pay the holders a premium price if such a security is retired early.

Call option right to buy 100 shares of a particular stock or stock index at a predetermined price before a preset deadline, in exchange for a premium.

Call protection aspects of the call provisions of an issue of callable securities that partially protect an investor against an issuer's call of the securities or act as a disincentive to the issuer's exercise of its call privileges. These features include restrictions on an issuer's right to call securities for a period of time after issuance, for example, an issue that cannot be called for ten years after issuance is said to have ten years of call protection; requirements that an issuer pay a premium redemption price for securities called within a certain period of time after issuance.

Capital gains difference between an asset's purchased price and selling price, when the difference is positive. A capital loss would be when the difference between an asset's purchase price and selling price is negative.

Capital stock stock authorized by a company's charter. The number and value of issued shares are normally shown, together with the number of shares authorized, in the capital accounts section of the balance sheet.

Cash account brokerage firm account whose transactions are settled on a cash basis. It is distinguished from a margin account, for which the broker extends credit.

Cash equivalents instruments or investments of such high liquidity and safety that they are virtually as good as cash.

Caveat emptor Latin for "let the buyer beware."

Central bank   country's bank that issues currency, administers monetary policy, holds deposits representing the reserves of other banks, and engages in other financial transactions for the government.

Certificate, stock   evidence of ownership of a corporation showing number of shares, name of issuer, and other information.

Certificate of deposit (CD)   debt instrument issued by a bank that usually pays interest. Maturities range from a few weeks to ten years or more.

Churning   excessive trading of a client's account by a broker. Churning is illegal.

Closed end fund   investment company with a limited number of shares outstanding. Such funds are often listed on an exchange, where they are traded like any other stock, often at less than their net asset value.

Collateral   assets pledged by a borrower to secure repayment of a loan or bond.

Collateralized mortgage obligation (CMO)   a form of *mortgage-backed security* that divides the cash flows from a pool of mortgages into multiple tranches. Each tranche is structured to have its own risk profile, yield, and expected maturity. Investors in the CMO can select the tranche that offers the characteristics meeting their needs.

Commercial paper   short-term obligations issued by banks, corporations, and other borrowers.

Committee on Uniform Securities Identification Procedures (CUSIP)   committee that assigns identifying numbers and codes for all securities.

Common stock   units of ownership of a public corporation. Owners typically are entitled to vote for directors and on other important matters as well as to receive dividends on their holdings.

Convertibles   corporate securities, usually preferred shares or bonds, that are exchangeable for a set number or another form of securities at a prestated price.

Corporate bonds   debt instrument used by a private

corporation, as distinct from one issued by a government agency or municipality.

Coupon term used colloquially to refer to a security's interest rate.

Coupon rate interest on a bond, expressed as an annual percentage of face value.

Covered option option contract backed by the shares underlying the option.

Credits loans, bonds, charge-account obligations, and open-account balances with commercial firms.

Currency risk risk that shifts in foreign exchange rates; such a shift may undermine the dollar value of overseas investments.

Current yield annual interest on a bond divided by the market price.

CUSIP identification number assigned to each fund by the Committee on Uniform Security Identification Procedures.

Custodian bank or other financial institution that holds stock certificates and other assets of a mutual fund, individual, or corporation.

Debenture general debt obligation backed only by the integrity of the borrower and documented by an agreement called an *indenture.*

Default failure of a debtor to make timely payments of interest and principal as they come due or to meet some other provision of a bond indenture.

Delinquency failure to make a payment on an obligation when due.

Deposited securities class of shares being offered in the ADR program, for example, ordinary, nonvoting, preferred, and so on.

Deregulation act of reducing government regulation in order to allow more free markets to create a more efficient marketplace. Some government oversight usually remains after deregulation.

Dilution effect on earnings per share and book value per share when all convertible securities are converted or all warrants or stock options are exercised.

Discount broker brokerage house that charges much lower commission rates than do full-service brokers.

Discount rate interest rate the Federal Reserve charges member banks for loans backed by government securities or other instruments as collateral.

Discretionary account account in which a broker has the power to buy or sell securities without the client's prior knowledge or consent.

Diversification concept of spreading one's money across different types of investments and/or issuers to potentially moderate the investment risk.

Dividend distribution of earnings to shareholders in an amount decided by the board of directors of the corporation.

Dow Jones Industrial Average (DJIA) unmanaged index of common stocks comprised of major industrial companies; it assumes reinvestment of dividends.

Efficient market theory thesis that market prices reflect the knowledge and expectations of all investors. Thus, any new development is quickly reflected in a firm's stock price.

Equity ownership interest possessed by shareholders in a corporation; stock as opposed to bonds.

Eurobond international bond issued and traded outside the country of the borrower and outside the regulations of a single country. Also called a *global bond*.

Eurodollar U.S. currency held in banks outside the United States, mainly in Europe, and commonly used for settling international transactions.

European depositary receipts usually listed on a European exchange, represented by a single global certificate, and deposited with a common depository on behalf of Euroclear and CEDEL. Ownership in the EDR is shown on the receipt, and transfers thereof are effected through records maintained by Euroclear and CEDEL. EDRs are not issued in the United States and therefore are not subject to regulation by the SEC.

Ex-dividend interval between the announcement and the payment of a dividend. Investors who buy shares during this interval are not entitled to the dividend.

Execution carrying out a trade.

Face value value that appears on the front, or face, of a bond that represents the amount the issuer promises to repay at maturity; also known as *par* or *principal* amount.

Fannie Mae common name for the Federal National Mortgage Association, a publicly owned corporation that purchases mortgages, mostly those backed by the Federal Housing Administration (FHA), and resells them to investors.

Financial future contract based on a financial instrument such as Treasury securities and foreign currencies.

Fiscal year (FY) accounting period covering 12 consecutive months, 52 consecutive weeks, or 365 consecutive days.

Flower bond type of U.S. government bond that, regardless of its cost price, is acceptable at par value in payment of estate taxes.

Freddie Mac common name for Federal Home Loan Mortgage Corporation, a publicly chartered agency that buys qualifying residential mortgages and packages them into new securities for sale to investors.

Front-end load sales charge applied to an investment at the time of initial purchase—on a mutual fund, for instance.

Full-service broker broker who provides a wide range of services to clients, including investment advice, and charges a full commission.

Futures market commodity exchange where futures contracts in different kinds of commodities and instruments are traded.

General obligation bond municipal backed by the full faith and credit of the issuing municipality.

Ginnie Mae common name for the Government National Mortgage Association, a U.S. agency that purchases mortgages from private lenders and packages them into securities called Ginnie Maes for sale to investors.

Global depositary receipts (GDR) depositary receipts that are eligible for settlement outside the United States. GDRs may be issued in New York, London, or Brussels and made eligible for use in U.S. markets.

Global funds broadly diversified funds that offer the highest level of diversification among international funds because they can invest anywhere in the world, including the United States.

Going public phrase used to describe a private company's first offering of shares to the investing public.

Good-till-canceled (GTC) order brokerage customer's order to buy or sell a security usually at a particular price that remains in effect until executed or canceled.

Growth stock common stock of a corporation that has shown faster than average gains in earnings over recent years.

Hedging strategy used to offset investment risk.

Holder of record owner of a company's securities as recorded on the books of that company or its transfer agent.

Index statistical composite that measures changes in the economy or in financial markets.

Indexing weighting an investment portfolio to match a broad-based index, such as the S&P 500, in order to match its performance.

Initial public offering (IPO) a corporation's first offering of stock to the public.

Insider person with access to key information before it is announced to the public.

Institutional investor financial or other institution, such as a pension fund, that buys and sells a large volume of securities.

Instrument legal document in which some contractual relationship is given formal expression or by which some right is granted.

Interest amount paid by a borrower as compensation for the use of borrowed money. This amount is generally expressed as an annual percentage of the principal amount.

Investment advisory service private entity providing investment advice for a fee. Such advisors must register with the SEC.

Investment grade term used to describe bonds suitable for purchase for prudent investors.

Issue date date on which a security is deemed to be issued or originated.

Issuer state, political subdivision, agency, or authority that borrows money through the sale of bonds or notes.

Junior issue debt or equity that is subordinate in claim to a senior security in terms of dividends, interest, or other matters.

Junk bond bond with a speculative credit rating of BB or lower and offering a higher rate of interest. These bonds are generally issued by new companies or those of questionable financial strength.

Letter security stock or bond that is not registered with the SEC and therefore cannot be sold in the public market.

Leveraged buyout takeover of a company using borrowed funds. Often the target company's assets serve as security for the loan taken out by the acquirer, who repays the loans out of the company's cash flow.

Limited partnership organization made up of general partners who manage a project and limited partners who invest money but who are not involved in management and thus have limited liability.

Limit order order to buy or sell a security at a specific price or better. The broker will execute the transaction only within the price restriction.

Liquid asset cash or an investment vehicle that is readily convertible into cash.

Liquidity ability to buy or sell an asset quickly or the ability to convert to cash quickly.

Listed security stock or bond that is traded on one of

the organized and registered exchanges in the United States.

Load sales charge paid by an investor who buys shares in a load mutual fund.

Long bond bond that matures in ten years or more; generally used to refer to the U.S. government 30-year bond.

Long position ownership of a security.

Margin account brokerage account allowing customers to buy securities with money borrowed from the broker. As regulated by the Federal Reserve Board, margin rates since 1945 have ranged from 50 percent to 100 percent of purchase price.

Margin call demand that a customer deposit enough money or securities to bring a margin account up to the minimum maintenance requirements, or percentage rate.

Market order order to buy or sell a security at the best available price.

Market price last recorded price at which a security was sold.

Market-value-weighted index index whose components are weighted according to the total market value of their outstanding shares.

Maturity date date on which the principal amount of a debt instrument becomes due or payable.

Medium-term bond bond with a maturity of two to ten years.

Merger combination of two or more companies, resulting in one larger company.

Money market market for short-term debt, such as negotiable certificates of deposit, commercial paper, Treasury bills, and so on.

Mortgage legal instrument that creates a lien upon real estate securing the payment of a specific debt.

Mortgage banker entity that originates mortgage loans, sells them to investors, and services the loans.

Mortgage loan loan secured by a mortgage.

Municipal bond debt obligation issued by a state or

local government. The funds raised may support a government's general financial needs or may be spent on a special project.

Mutual fund fund operated by an investment company that invests money raised from investors in stocks, bonds, and other securities. These funds offer investors diversification and professional management and charge a management fee.

Nasdaq National Association of Securities Dealers Automated Quotations system.

National Association of Securities Dealers (NASD) nonprofit organization that includes virtually all investment banking houses and firms dealing in the over-the-counter market.

National Securities Clearing Corporation (NSCC) organization through which brokerage firms, exchanges, and other financial institutions reconcile accounts with each other.

New York Stock Exchange (NYSE) oldest (1792) and largest stock exchange in the United States; also known as the *Big Board* and *The Exchange*.

No-load fund mutual fund that does not levy any sales charges or commissions, but charges other annual fees.

Nonrecurring charge one-time expense or write-off appearing in a company's financial statements.

Odd lot securities trade made for less than the normal trading unit (termed a round lot). In most, but not all, stock trading, less than 100 shares is considered an odd lot.

Offer price at which a seller will sell a security.

Offshore term used in the United States for any financial organization that has its headquarters outside the country.

Open interest total number of contracts in a commodity or options market that are still open, that have not been exercised, closed out, or allowed to expire.

Option in general, the right to buy or sell property that is granted in exchange for an agreed-upon sum. If the right is not exercised after a specified period, the option expires and is thus worthless.

Option writer individual or financial institution that sells put or call options.

Original face face value or original amount of a security on its issue date.

Over-the-counter (OTC) term for a stock that is not listed or traded on an organized exchange but in a market in which transactions are conducted through a telephone and computer network linking dealers throughout the country.

Par price equal to the face amount of a security, as distinct from its market value. On a debt security, the par or face value is the amount the investor has been promised to receive from the issuer at maturity.

Pass-through security security that passes income from debtor through intermediaries to investors. The most common form is a mortgage-backed security.

Paying agent entity responsible for making the payment of interest and principal to bondholders on behalf of the bond's issuer.

Payment date date on which actual principal and interest payments are paid to the registered owner of a security.

Penny stock stock that typically sells for less than $1 per share, and is issued by companies with a short or erratic history of revenues.

Pink sheets daily publication of the National Quotation Bureau that lists the bid and ask prices of thousands of OTC stocks not on the Nasdaq system.

Point in bonds quotations, 1 percent (a basis point is 0.01%); in stocks, $1.

Pool collection of mortgage loans assembled by an originator or master servicer as the basis for a security. Ginnie Mae, Fannie Mae, or Freddie Mac pass-through securities are identified by a number assigned by the issuing agency.

Preemptive right right giving existing stockholders the opportunity to purchase shares of a new issue before it is offered to others.

Preferred stock class of capital stock that pays dividends at a specified rate and has preference over common stock in the payment of dividends and liquidation of assets, but does not ordinarily carry voting rights.

Preliminary prospectus first document released by the underwriter of a new issue to prospective investors.

Pretax rate of return rate of return that is earned on your investments or savings before applicable federal, state, and local income taxes are subtracted.

Prepayment unscheduled partial or complete payment of the principal amount outstanding on a debt obligation before it is due.

Price dollar amount to be paid for a security, stated as a percentage of its face value or par in the case of debt securities.

Price earnings (PE) ratio price of a stock divided by its annual earnings per share.

Price-weighted index index in which component stocks are weighted by their price.

Prime rate interest rate banks charge to their most creditworthy customers. The prime rate serves as a basis for the determination of other interest rates, including some mortgage rates.

Principal face amount of a bond, exclusive of accrued interest, if any, and payable at maturity. With mortgage securities, principal refers to the amount outstanding on the mortgage loans.

Program trading computer-directed sale or purchase of a basket of stocks equivalent to an index such as the S&P 500.

Prospectus formal written offer to sell securities that sets forth the plan for a proposed business enterprise or the facts concerning an existing business. Prospectuses are also issued by mutual funds.

Put option contract that grants an investor the right to sell at a specified price a specified number of shares by a certain date.

Random walk theory about the movement of stock and

commodity futures price hypothesizing that past prices are of no use in forecasting future price movements. According to this theory, stock prices react to information coming to the market in a random fashion.

Rate of return gain or loss generated from an investment over a specified period of time; also referred to as *total return,* it includes the change in the value of a security plus all interest, dividends, and capital gains distributions generated by holding that security.

Ratings designations used by investors' services to give relative indications of credit quality.

Real estate investment trust (REIT) a company, usually traded publicly, that manages a portfolio of real estate in order to earn profits for shareholders.

Real interest rate current interest rate minus inflation rate.

Record date date for determining the owner entitled to the next scheduled payment of principal or interest on a mortgage security.

Regional stock exchanges organized national securities exchanges located outside New York City.

Registered owner name in which a security is registered, as stated on the certificate or on the books of the paying agent. P&I payments are made to the registered owner on the record date.

Repurchase agreement (REPO) agreement between a seller and a buyer—usually of U.S. government securities—whereby the seller agrees to repurchase the securities at an agreed-upon price and, usually, at a stated time.

Revenue anticipation note (RAN) short-term debt issue of a municipality that is to be repaid out of anticipated revenues such as sales taxes.

Reverse split procedure whereby a corporation reduces the number of its shares outstanding by exchanging, for example, one share for every ten shares then issued.

Rights offering offering of common stock to existing shareholders who hold rights that entitle them to buy newly issued shares at a discount from the market price.

Risk tolerance one's comfort level with fluctuations in the value of investments and the potential for loss.

Round lot generally accepted unit of trading on a securities exchange; typically, 100 shares of stock or $1,000 (par value) in bonds.

Safekeeping storage and protection of customers' securities, typically held in a vault, provided as a service by a bank or institution acting as agent for the customer.

Sallie Mae Student Loan Marketing Association, a publicly traded corporation that administers federally guaranteed student loans.

Savings bond U.S. government bond, issued at a discount, in denominations ranging from $50 to $10,000. Interest paid is exempt from state and local taxes.

Secondary distribution public sale of previously issued securities by large investors.

Securities analyst individual who performs investment research and examines the financial condition of a company or group of companies in an industry and in the context of the securities market.

Securities and Exchange Commission (SEC) federal agency created by the Securities Exchange Act of 1934 to administer that act and the Securities Act of 1933. The SEC is the most important agency engaged in the regulation of the securities markets.

Securities Industry Association (SIA) trade group that represents broker-dealers.

Securities Investor Protection Corporation (SIPC) nonprofit corporation established by Congress that insures the securities and cash in the customer accounts of member brokerage firms against failure of those firms, up to $500,000.

Senior debt loans or debt securities that have claims prior to junior obligations and equity on a corporation's assets in the event of liquidation.

Servicing collection and aggregation of principal, interest, and escrow payments on mortgage loans and mortgage securities, as well as certain operational procedures such as accounting, bookkeeping, insurance, tax records, loan payment follow-up, delinquency loan follow-up, and loan analysis. The party providing servicing, the servicer, receives a servicing fee.

Settlement date date agreed upon by the parties to a transaction for the delivery of securities and payment of funds. This may vary from other bonds.

Shareholder owner of one or more shares of stock in a corporation or one or more shares or units of a mutual fund. Shareholder rights can vary according to the articles of incorporation or the by-laws of a particular company.

Shelf registration term used to describe the SEC procedure that allows corporations to comply with registration requirements up to two years prior to a public offering of securities.

Short sale sale of a security or a commodity futures contract not owned by the seller. An investor borrows stock for delivery at the time of the short sale, hoping to buy back that stock later at a lower price. A commodity sold short represents a promise to deliver that commodity at a set price on a set future date.

Short-term investment that matures in a year or less.

Small-cap stocks investment categorization based on the market capitalization of a company.

Small investor individual investor who buys small amounts of stocks or bonds, often in odd lot quantities.

Spot market commodities market in which goods are sold for cash and delivered immediately.

Standard & Poor's 500 broad-based measurement of changes in stock market conditions based on the average performance of 500 widely held common stocks.

Stock funds mutual funds that invest primarily in stocks. They offer diversification by investing in a number of different companies or industries, according to guidelines set in the funds' prospectuses. Stock funds are usually categorized by the types of stocks they invest in; for example, growth funds, small capitalization funds, and international funds. Stock funds are not FDIC insured, and involve risk to principal.

Stop-limit order   order to a securities broker with instructions to buy or sell at a specified price or better.

Stop-loss order   order to a securities broker that sets the selling price of a stock below the current market price; used both to stop losses and protect profits.

Subsidiary   company of which more than 50 percent of the voting shares are owned by another corporation.

Takeover   change in the controlling interest of a corporation, through a friendly acquisition or merger or through an unfriendly bid or tender offer.

Tax deferred   term that refers to investments or accounts whose earnings are not taxed until some time in the future, generally when earnings are withdrawn.

Tax-exempt security   financial instrument whose interest is exempt from taxation by federal, state, and/or local government.

TIGR   Treasury Investors Growth Receipt, a form of zero coupon security first created by the brokerage firm of Merrill Lynch.

Trade date   day on which a security or a commodity future trade actually takes place.

Tranche   *see* Collateralized Mortgage Obligation (CMO).

Transfer agent   party appointed to maintain records of securities owners, to cancel and issue certificates, and to address issues arising from lost, destroyed, or stolen certificates.

Treasuries   negotiable debt obligations of the U.S. government, secured by its full faith and credit and issued at various schedules and maturities.

Treasury bills   short-term securities with maturities of one year or less.

Treasury bonds   long-term debt instruments with maturities of ten years or longer.

Treasury notes   intermediate securities with maturities of from one to ten years.

Underwriter   investment banker who, singly or as a

member of an underwriting group or syndicate, agrees to purchase a new issue of securities from an issuer and resell the securities to investors.

Unit investment trust investment company that purchases a fixed portfolio of income-producing securities, such as bonds, mortgage-backed securities, or preferred stock. Units in the trust are sold to investors, who receive a proportional interest in both the principal and the income portion of the portfolio.

Unlisted security security that is not listed on an organized stock exchange.

U.S. government securities *see* Treasuries.

Variable annuity life insurance annuity contract whose value fluctuates with that of an underlying securities portfolio or other index of performance.

Venture capital important source of financing for start-up companies; also called *risk capital.*

Warrant type of security, usually issued together with a bond or preferred stock, that entitles the holder to buy a proportionate amount of common stock at a specified price, usually higher than the market price at the time of issuance, for a period of years or to perpetuity.

When issued transaction made conditionally because a security, although authorized, has not yet been issued.

Widow-and-orphan stock stock that pays high dividends and is very safe.

Yield to call the same as *yield to maturity* with the exception that the yield to call calculation assumes that the bond will be redeemed by the issuer on the first call date and at the specified call price.

Yield to maturity (YTM) the rate of return an investor will receive if a long-term, interest-bearing investment, such as a bond, is held to its maturity date.

Zero-coupon security security that makes no periodic interest payments but instead is sold at a deep discount from its face value. The buyer receives the rate of return by the gradual appreciation of the security, which is redeemed at face value on a specified maturity date.

INDEX